WINELANDS
of COLORADO

*An intimate portrait
of winemaking in a rugged land*

WINELANDS of COLORADO

An intimate portrait
of winemaking in a rugged land

text by

Christina Holbrook

with photography by

Marc Hoberman

HOBERMAN
PHOTOGRAPHIC PUBLISHERS
CAPE TOWN – LONDON – MIAMI

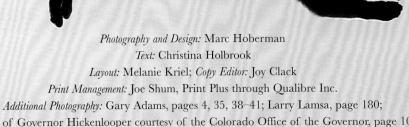

Photography and Design: Marc Hoberman
Text: Christina Holbrook
Layout: Melanie Kriel; *Copy Editor:* Joy Clack
Print Management: Joe Shum, Print Plus through Qualibre Inc.
Additional Photography: Gary Adams, pages 4, 35, 38–41; Larry Lamsa, page 180;
Photo of Governor Hickenlooper courtesy of the Colorado Office of the Governor, page 10;
Photo of Warren Winiarski by Bob McClenahan, courtesy of Arcadia Vineyard, page 12;
Photo of Marc Hoberman by Grace Hutton, page 15

www.hobermancollection.com

ISBN: 978-1-919939-96-4

Winelands of Colorado is published by HOBERMAN
10 Frazzitta Business Park, Cape Town, South Africa 7441
Telephone: +27 (21) 551 0270
Email: office@hobermancollection.com

Agents and Distributors
United States and International
Perseus Distribution
1400 Broadway, Suite 520
New York, NY 10018
Tel: (212) 714-9000
Email: client.info@perseusbooks.com

*A special thank you to Wine Country Inn
for their sterling support of this project.
Our Palisade home away from home!*

*A heartfelt thank you to all the participants in this book for their support and
friendship. Additional thank you for the support of Laurence Bard, Magda Bosch,
Dr Horst Caspari, Leslie Coggan, Sid Desalvo, Alan Dulit, Chris Epic, Governor
John Hickenlooper, Lulu Hunt, Heather Jarvis, Ian Kelley, Molly Kreck,
Marisol Montoya, John Sabal, Holly Shrewsbury, Cassidee Shull, Anne Tally,
Richard and Jean Tally, Laura Warren, Warren Winiarski and Ruca Wonai.*

Leaping mountain lion! Late evening action in the mountains of Canyon of the Ancients

Printed in China

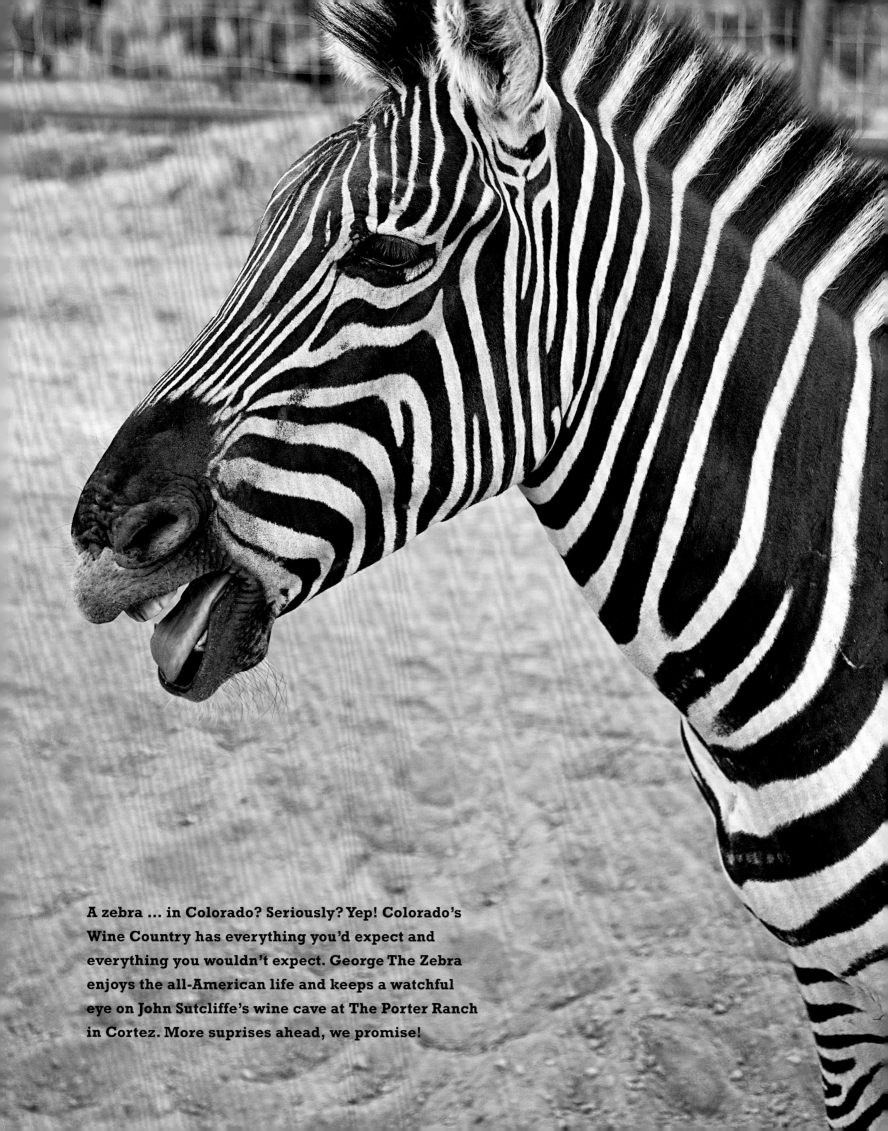

A zebra … in Colorado? Seriously? Yep! Colorado's Wine Country has everything you'd expect and everything you wouldn't expect. George The Zebra enjoys the all-American life and keeps a watchful eye on John Sutcliffe's wine cave at The Porter Ranch in Cortez. More suprises ahead, we promise!

Contents

ROCKY MOUNTA

Wo

Eagle

GRAND VALLEY AVA

Loma

Fruita

Palisade

Aspen

Grand Junction

Grand Mesa

Cedaredge

Paonia

DELTA

Hotchkiss

Crested Bu

WEST ELKS AVA

Gunnison

MONTROSE

Telluride

Dolores

Cortez

THE FOUR CORNERS

Durango

Mesa Verde

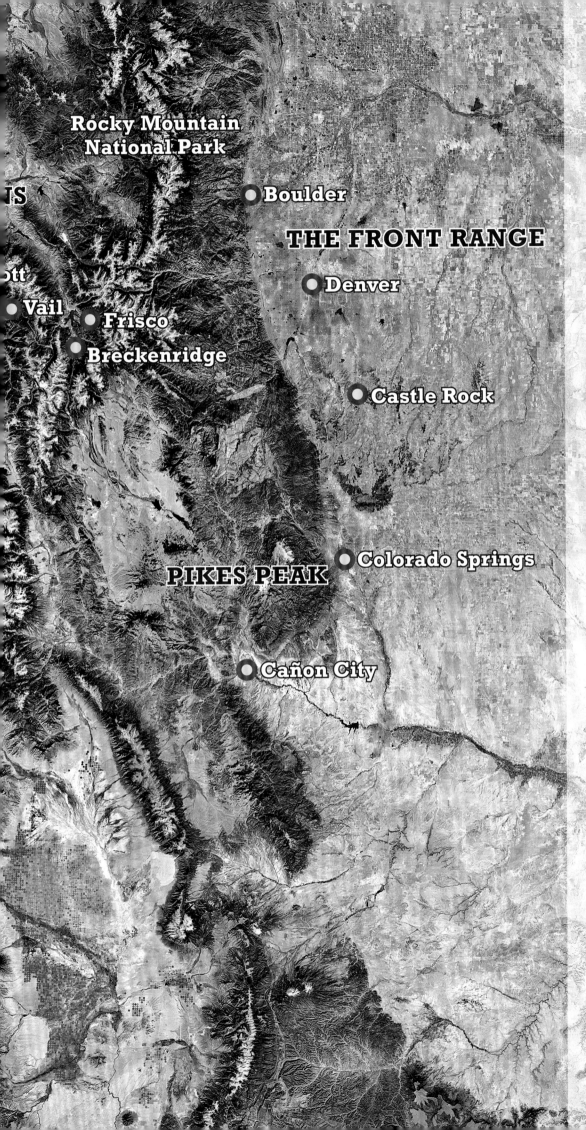

Rocky Mountain
National Park

THE FRONT RANGE

● Boulder

IS

ott

● Vail

● Frisco

● Breckenridge

● Denver

● Castle Rock

PIKES PEAK

● Colorado Springs

● Cañon City

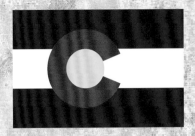

COLORADO

Nil sine numine

Nothing without Providence

Nickname The Centennial State

Capital Denver

Total Area 104,094 sq mi (269,837 km²)

Highest Point Mount Elbert (Lake County)
144,440 ft (4,401.2 m)

Lowest Point Arikaree River
3,317 ft (1,011 m)

Population 5,456,574 (2015 est)

Grapes Produced Cabernet Franc,
Cabernet Sauvignon, Chambourcin,
Chardonel, Chardonnay, Cinsault,
Gewürztraminer, Lemberger, Marechal
Foch, Merlot, Muscat Canelli, Orange
Muscat, Petit Verdot, Pinot Gris, Pinot
Noir, Riesling, Sangiovese, Sauvignon
Blanc, Sémillon, Seyval Blanc, Syrah,
Viognier, Zinfandel

Foreword

by John Hickenlooper, Governor of Colorado

Colorado's modern history of winemaking began nearly 50 years ago with a few intrepid pioneers and a bold undertaking to re-establish vineyards in the Grand Valley where, early in the 20th century, vines had been destroyed during Prohibition. Today Colorado boasts over 140 wineries across the state – from the desert mesas of Cortez to high-altitude Paonia; from the fertile valleys of Palisade to the busy urban neighborhoods of downtown Denver. With two American Viticultural Areas located within its borders, Colorado is recognized as having terrain suitable for growing the classic European varieties, the "noble grapes". In addition, innovative winemakers are experimenting with unusual blends, as well as the production of ciders, meads and fruit wines. Wine connoisseurs and visitors to Colorado are beginning to discover what many locals already know: today, world-class wines are being produced (and enjoyed!) in the State of Colorado. Hoberman and Holbrook's *Winelands of Colorado* takes the reader on a beautiful photographic tour of wine-producing regions throughout the state, from remote vineyards where grapes are grown at the highest elevation in the northern hemisphere, to pastoral sweeps of vines that bring to mind the South of France. Above all, here are the stories of Colorado's winemakers, an inside look at the passion and dedication that drive them to create wine in this rugged, remarkable land. Welcome to the winelands of Colorado. I invite you to raise a glass to Colorado wines, and enjoy your journey.

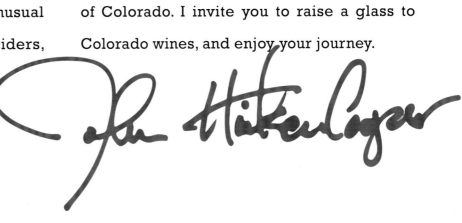

Introduction

by Warren Winiarski

Having been invited to write the introduction for this impressive and informative book on the new wines of Colorado, I accepted with pleasure for reasons you should know. In 1968, Dr Gerald Ivancie (the late Denver periodontist) asked me to be his consultant and winemaker for a pioneering initiative to establish the third winery in the state. It would be a Colorado winery with a difference. He proposed that the winery would be the first of others to follow, he hoped, for the production of *Vitis vinifera*, the species of European grapes which produce the world's great wines. He thought that Colorado was ready and able to make such wine. At the time, I had been involved with the first two years of winemaking at another pioneering venture, the new Robert Mondavi winery in the Napa Valley, and I loved the determination to make wines of the highest quality by Robert Mondavi, his sons and daughter. But the challenge of another such effort in an untried area led me to take up the call of Colorado. The first wines were made from grapes grown in California. However, we immediately began to explore the interest of growers in the Grand Valley to convert their orchards into vineyards so that they would have an opportunity to be the leading edge, within Colorado, for the bounding wine developments in the country. Those early days were satisfying for they planted some of the seeds for what was to come, and I was happy to have contributed my small part. Not long after, Colorado Mountain Vineyards (which today operates as Colorado Cellars) was established. It is the winery, I believe, that would successfully create the first unified endeavor producing wine from Colorado grapes. After the partnership was formed for Stag's Leap Wine Cellars and vineyard in 1970, I would no longer have the ability to carry on for Dr Ivancie since my time was taken up in the Napa Valley. In 2014, I was invited to be a tasting judge of Colorado wines at the Annual Governor's Cup Competition in Denver. And what a thrill it was to see how far and fast Colorado wines have achieved general excellence in all categories. It is clear that the state's growers and wineries have learned how to get very good outcomes from the specific challenges of Colorado climate and mountain settings – and they have formed their lovely, authentic voice for the place that they are in. They have not aimed to duplicate, with their varietal wines, the varietal "look" that belongs to other places and climates. For example, Cabernet Sauvignon has a lighter, subtler texture in Colorado than

Warren Winiarski is the founder of Stag's Leap Wine Cellars in Napa Valley. Stag's Leap, widely recognized as one of the premier wineries in the world, achieved international acclaim when its 1973 Cabernet Sauvignon was rated the top red wine at the now historic Judgment of Paris in 1976. This award effectively put California wines – and by extension, American wines – on the map

in places where there are different growing conditions. Colorado is a high mountain terroir! Cabernet Franc has a leaner but very complete structure when grown at these high altitudes. This is one of the best red wines for the Colorado conditions; it always does well in the tastings I have attended – a perfect friend with food. The white wines in general have a very appealing delicacy and freshness. Hoberman and Holbrook's *Winelands of Colorado* beautifully captures the "sense" of the different places it portrays with its photos and text. From grand to modest, you meet the people, you see where they make their wines, and in some cases, see the vines they love. They are the winemakers and grape growers who are living the life of the vine in this beautiful state. Some are pioneers in fact, but all are pioneers in spirit. For they are all searching and they are all brave. Their challenges are not small because newness confronts them at many turns in their journey to the promised land

14

A Note on Photography

by Marc Hoberman

Wine country is always an exciting place to photograph. My photographic travels take me to all sorts of destinations – from deserts to jungles, big cities to wildlife safaris, but there is something special about photographing in wine country. Maybe it's the light (tip #1: light that makes good wine makes good photographs), maybe it's the dramatic landscapes (tip #2: landscapes that make for good wine, make good photographs), maybe it's the enthralling opportunity for soulful portraits (tip #3: people who make good wine, make for good photographs). No pun intended but you can start to see the picture! Colorado's

wine country is unique in what it has to offer the photographer – a heady mix of majestic mountains, lush vistas, arid outback, elks, marmots, cowboys, rock art, dramatic clouds, powdery snow, glassy lakes … and an extensive list of further adjectives and nouns that would make any photographer happily wake up before dawn. For those who are interested, these are some of my tips for your own photographic adventure. With the exception of shooting in dark cellars, leave your tripod at home, it only gets in the way of spontaneity; and

while you're at it, leave your flash at home too – it removes all the beautiful subtleties of light that nature provides. I can highly recommend a loupe for cutting out the ambient light while looking at your LCD screen, plus it makes you look fancier than a big lens does! The camera that I use is a Canon 1DX and the lens that I found most useful on this trip was a 24mm-70mm 2.8 (high-speed lenses are well worth the investment). If you are photographing people my two suggestions are: talk the whole time while you are photographing, that is the only way you will get a true personality coming through in your photo (and fascinatingly it becomes a portrait of both them and you!). Secondly, and this goes for pretty much everything, don't be scared to press the shutter 100 times. Your third shot may be perfect, your 40th may be even more perfect, the effort is always rewarded. I hope the photographs in this book convey the passion that I have for Colorado's wine country, and I hope that there is a photograph somewhere in these pages that makes you want to pick up your camera and explore!

— THE FOUR CORNERS —

The southwest corner of Colorado butts up against Utah, Arizona, and New Mexico to form a region known as The Four Corners. It is a land that is rural, rugged and dry, characterized by ochre bluffs and sagebrush. Ancient cave dwellings and mysterious prehistoric petroglyphs attract many adventurous visitors to these canyons and mesas. From the northeast, travelers to The Four Corners follow a route that winds through the spectacular San Juan Mountains; Trail of the Ancients and the Old Spanish Trail lead into the region from the west and south. In prehistoric times, hunter-gatherer tribes roamed this region. These were the ancient ancestors to the Ute and Navajo. By 750 CE the Pueblo had begun to create dwellings in and around Mesa Verde; they vanished mysteriously by 1300 CE leaving behind the spectacular cliff dwellings at Mesa Verde. Today traces of these ancient civilizations exist in the form of dwellings, kiva, ruins and towers – alongside the vibrant modern cultures of the region's Native Americans. In recent years, the region has seen the arrival of a new generation of farmers and ranchers concerned with sustainable farming and growing practices. Several important wineries also make their home in this region. Still, with temperatures that can hit a high of 100 degrees in summer and drop more than 30 degrees overnight, it would be fair to say that only the most hardy – or, some might say, foolhardy – would attempt to wrest a living from this unforgiving land. The largest town in the region is Durango, where restaurants, shops, and hotels give a classic Western flavor. Durango is also the hub of the historic Durango–Silverton rail line, which is still in use today taking visitors north to the old mining town of Silverton. Cortez lies to the west of Durango, were local shops and modern farm-to-table restaurants lie just a few miles from rugged McElmo Canyon and Hovenweep National Monument. And an hour from Cortez, towards Dolores and the hot springs of Dunton, the landscape shifts from high desert to aspen and birch. McElmo Canyon and Canyon of the Ancients is the setting for the remote Sutcliffe Vineyards. The altitude is approximately 5,200 feet and the soil is sandy loam. With less than 13 inches of rainfall annually, growers and winemakers carefully calibrate the amount of irrigation necessary. In this high desert territory, Cabernet Sauvignon, Petit Verdot, Merlot, Syrah and Chardonnay grow under the watchful eye of the winemakers.

 *In prehistoric times, hunter-gatherer tribes roamed this region. These were the ancient ancestors to the Ute and Navajo. Today farmers, ranchers, and winemakers make this land their home.*

Sutcliffe Vineyards

Est. 1995

In this timeless landscape, where man and animal have roamed the desert hills for millennia, winemaker John Sutcliffe has chosen to dedicate himself to creating a green oasis of vineyards and farmland.

Sutcliffe Vineyards lies in the remote southwest corner of Montezuma County, Colorado, bordered by the Ute Mountain Ute Reservation to the south, and the Utah state line 12 miles to the east. In this relentlessly harsh and untamed desert climate, with blistering summers and icy winters, ever-charismatic winemaker John Sutcliffe has devoted himself to creating world-class wines – and an unrivaled experience for the adventurous visitor to his beautiful and secluded McElmo Canyon.

Owner John Sutcliffe

Winemaker Joe Buckel

Assistant Winemakers Jesus Castillo and David Culliton

Coordinates 37°20'19.9"N 108°49'26.5"W

Altitude 5,340 ft

Annual Rainfall Liquid precipitation 16.4" (13" rain; 34" snow)

Dominant Soil Type Sandy loam

Prominent Wines Chardonnay, Sauvignon Blanc, Merlot, Cinsaut, Cabernet Franc, Cabernet Sauvignon, and Syrah

Annual Production 5,000 cases

Wine Tasting Available 7 days a week, 12pm to 5pm

Notable Awards 90pt Ratings for 3 different varietals in 2014 from the *Wine Enthusiast*: Cabernet Franc, Syrah, and Chardonnay. Editors' Choice, the *Wine Enthusiast*: Viognier in 2014. 2016 Governor's Cup Gold Medal: Chardonnay 2015

Website www.sutcliffewines.com

It is hard not to get swept up in the romance of the outlandish challenge that John Sutcliffe has given himself: create world-class wines in the middle of a desert that outwitted even the ancient Pueblo people. By the time Sutcliffe moved to southwest Colorado, he had served in the British Military and created or managed over 22 award-winning restaurants – including the famed Tavern on the Green in New York City. He is a man not easily intimidated by hard work or unlikely prospects.

In 1989 he purchased property in McElmo Canyon. He called it Battlerock Ranch in honor of the stunning red sandstone edifice that towers over the farm. Legend has it that ancient Navajo tribes threw themselves from this precipice in desperation and defiance rather than be captured by Ute warriors. Gaining the trust and respect of ranchers and Native American locals, Sutcliffe began to create his oasis in the desert – planting orchards and hay and raising livestock. In 1995 the first vines were planted on the farm, establishing Sutcliffe Vineyards, 1999 saw the first harvest, and in 2001 the first vintage was released.

Winemaker Joe Buckel arrived in 2008 from California's Sonoma County. Working together, and with the advice and good sense of Jesus Castillo and David Culliton, Buckel and Sutcliffe have developed wines that are exquisitely balanced and intended to be paired with food. Their hard work has not gone unnoticed: in 2014 the *Wine Enthusiast* gave Sutcliffe Vineyards' Merlot, Syrah, and Cabernet Franc 90 point ratings. Sutcliffe wines consistently show up on the lists of restaurants and resorts within Colorado – as well as Los Angeles, New York City, and even London.

McElmo Canyon and neighboring Canyon of the Ancients offer a wealth of opportunities to explore one of the most archeologically rich regions in the world. Nearby Hovenweep National Monument includes prehistoric villages and towers that can be explored on foot; and Sand Canyon Trail is a popular loop for mountain bikers, passing by Puebloan ruins amid gorgeous desert scenery. The region's Mesa Verde National Park will also provide visitors with spectacular ancient ruins.

Ascending the northern flank of the Battlerock, with the farm and vineyard below, left. At right, *Sutcliffe is the consummate host at the vineyard.*

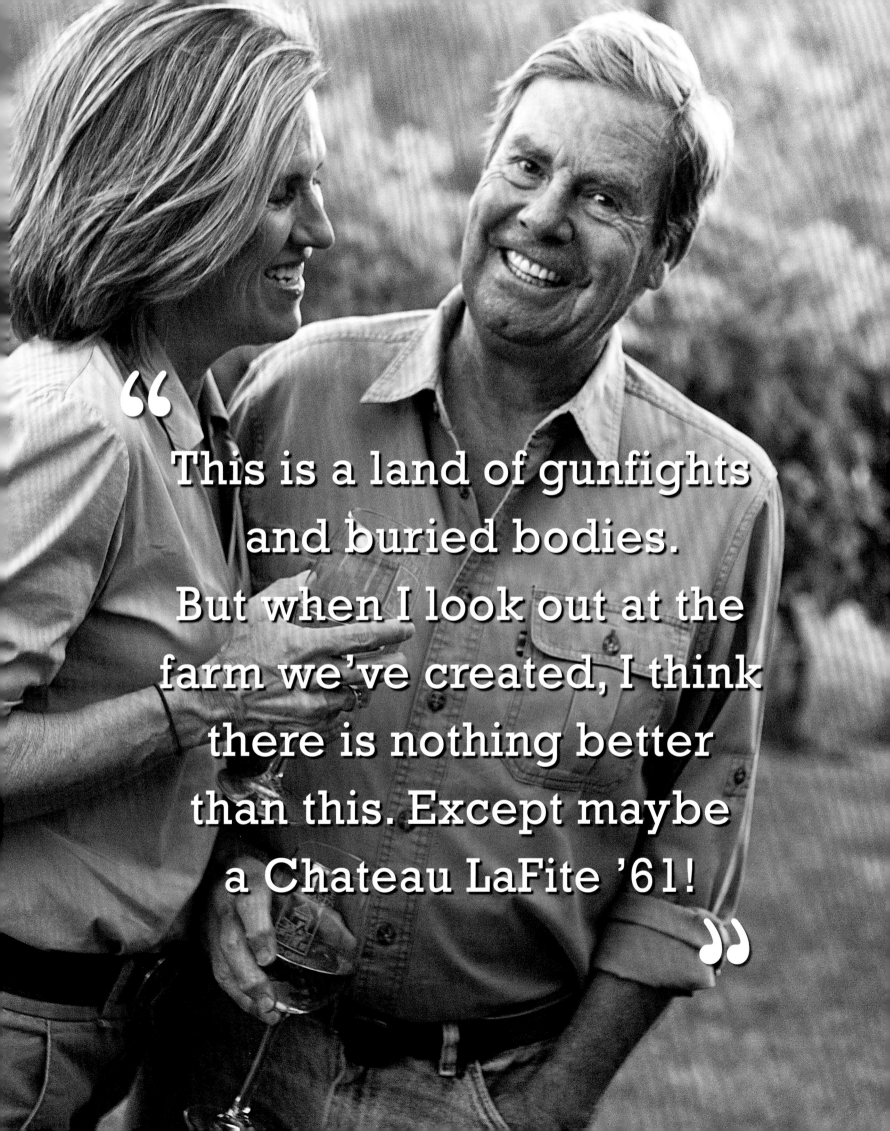

" This is a land of gunfights and buried bodies. But when I look out at the farm we've created, I think there is nothing better than this. Except maybe a Chateau LaFite '61! "

Dawn breaks and light spills over the ancient desert peaks, illuminating the red rock canyons and the great Battlerock overlooking the vineyard and farm. By midday, the heat will be intense, and vine-covered trellises offer a shady respite for winetasters.

Arriving from Sonoma County, winemaker Joe Buckel (left) was initially taken aback by the challenge of growing grapes in the harsh desert conditions of Colorado. For 10 years he has persevered to create wines that would match the grand spirit of Battlerock Ranch. Today, the wines from Sutcliffe Vineyards are known for their balance, focus, and finish. The strong UV rays at high altitude create grapes with thick skins, leading to smoother tannins in the red wine varietals, while the whites possess a distinct crispness and minerality.

Herds of cattle wander freely, enjoying the lush grass and the pleasant shade beneath groves of aspen trees, in the higher elevations near Dunton Hot Springs resort.

Dunton Hot Springs Resort
DOLORES

Take a left outside the town of Dolores. As the dirt
road climbs through shimmering aspens, the air
begins to cool. The view opens up to a picturesque
19th-century mining town, and you'll wonder if
you've stepped back in time. You've arrived at
Dunton Hot Springs, today restored and reimagined
as a rustic luxury resort. This dance hall dates
from the late 1800s and now serves as a bathhouse
where guests can enjoy the natural hot springs.

Butch Cassidy's Bar

In 1885, Dunton was established as a mining camp in the lonely, uninhabited mountains west of Telluride. This wild and lawless location made it the perfect hideout for outlaws such as Butch Cassidy, who reportedly holed up in Dunton after robbing the San Miguel Valley Bank in Telluride. The bar at Dunton Hot Springs resort, dating from the original mining days, still bears Butch Cassidy's carved signature.

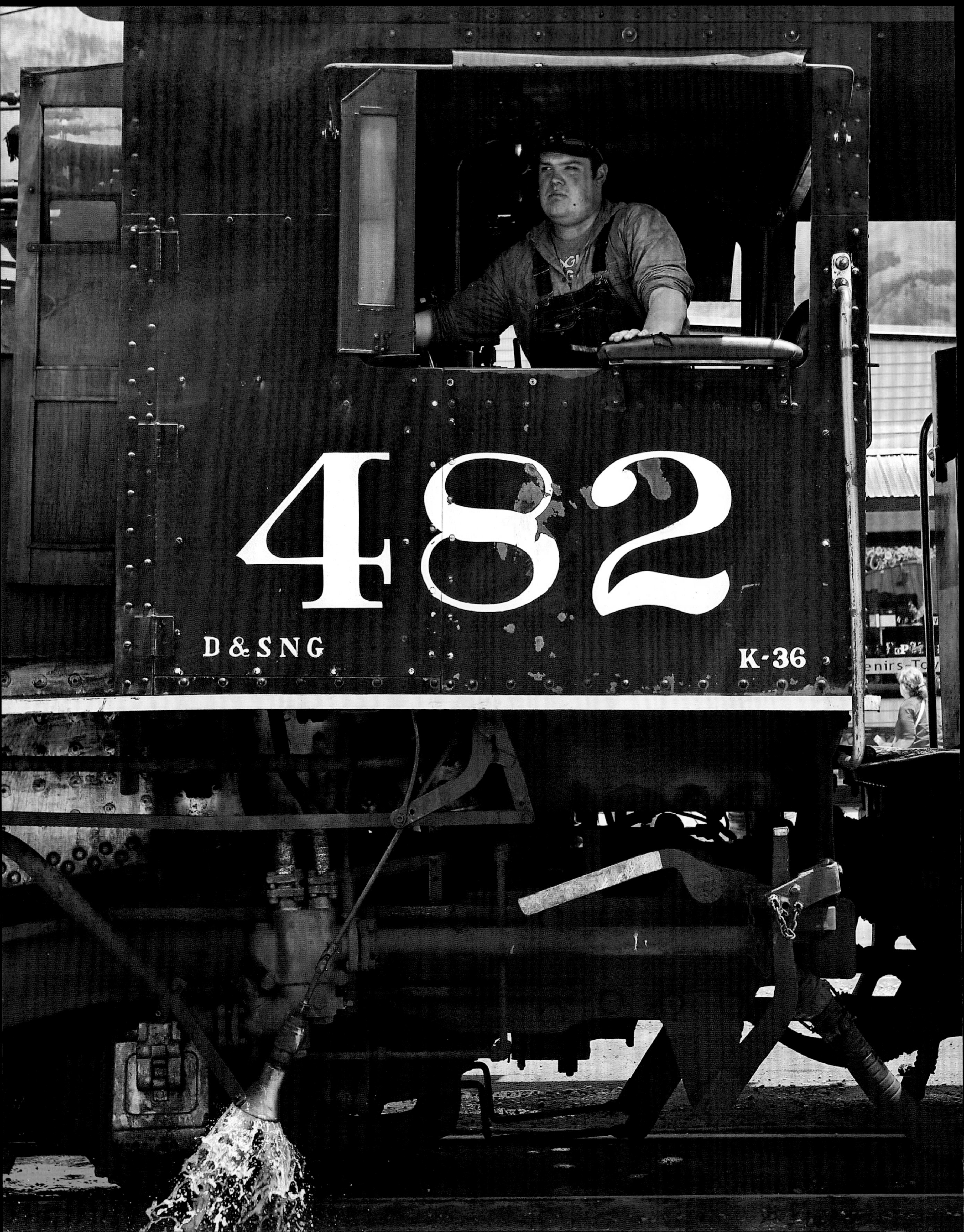
482
D&SNG
K-36

DURANGO & SILVERTON NARROW GAUGE RAILWAY TRAIN

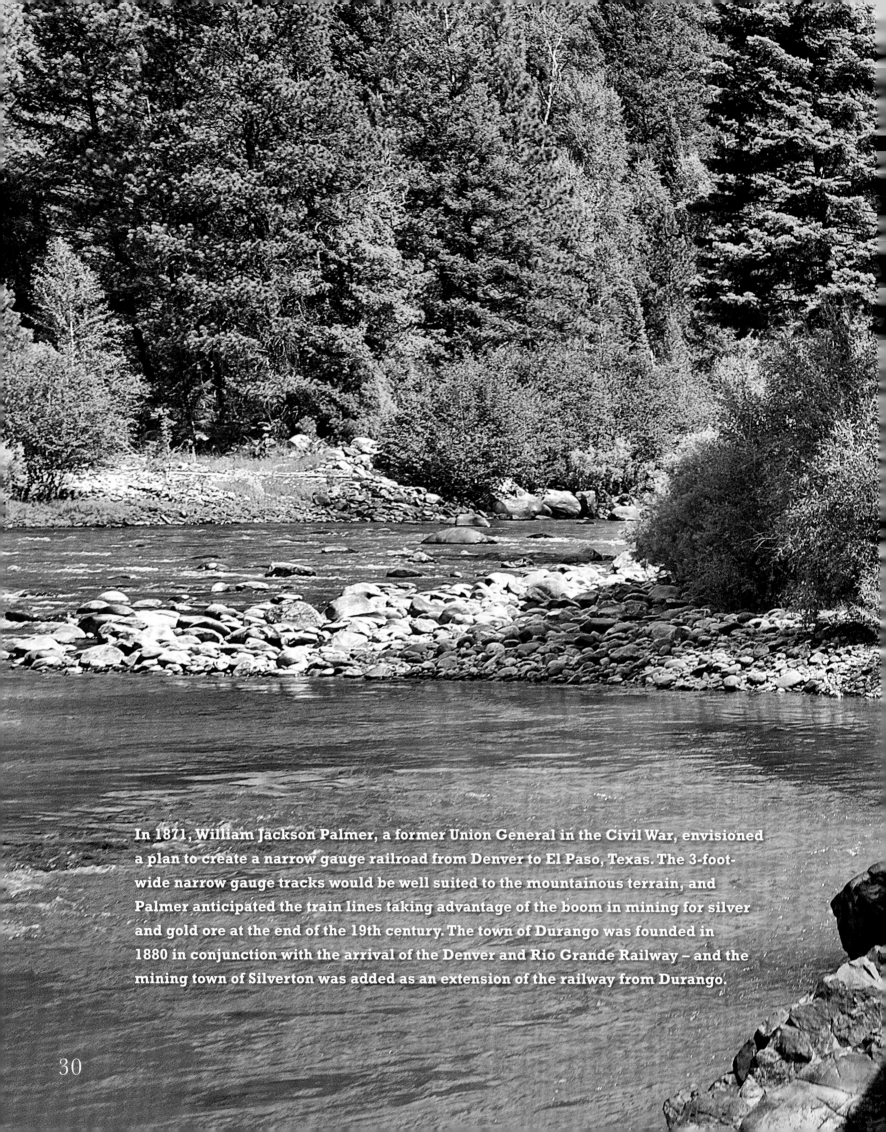

In 1871, William Jackson Palmer, a former Union General in the Civil War, envisioned a plan to create a narrow gauge railroad from Denver to El Paso, Texas. The 3-foot-wide narrow gauge tracks would be well suited to the mountainous terrain, and Palmer anticipated the train lines taking advantage of the boom in mining for silver and gold ore at the end of the 19th century. The town of Durango was founded in 1880 in conjunction with the arrival of the Denver and Rio Grande Railway – and the mining town of Silverton was added as an extension of the railway from Durango.

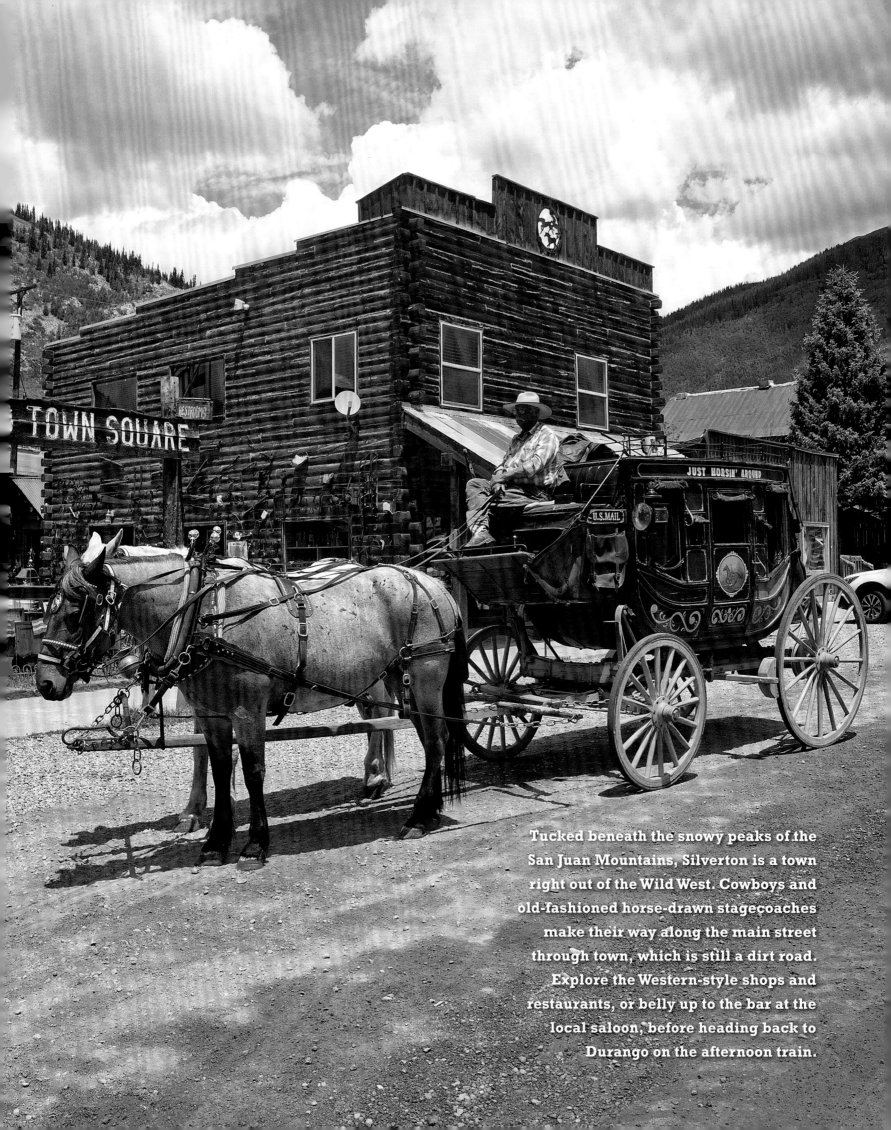

Tucked beneath the snowy peaks of the San Juan Mountains, Silverton is a town right out of the Wild West. Cowboys and old-fashioned horse-drawn stagecoaches make their way along the main street through town, which is still a dirt road. Explore the Western-style shops and restaurants, or belly up to the bar at the local saloon, before heading back to Durango on the afternoon train.

Canyon of the Ancients Guest Ranch

This historic guest ranch with private cabins is located along the winding route through rugged McElmo Canyon, which was once referred to as "Robbers Path", where outlaws such as Butch Cassidy are rumored to have stashed their treasure.

While guests will feel they have discovered a remote hideaway, in fact the Canyon of the Ancients Guest Ranch is within close proximity to Durango, Cortez, and the ruins at Mesa Verde. Sutcliffe Vineyards, also in McElmo Canyon, is approximately five miles to the east. Surrounding the ranch is Canyon of the Ancients National Monument, a landscape rich in prehistoric archeological sites and petroglyph drawings. Here the ancient Pueblo people lived, and today visitors wishing to explore the area on foot, mountain bike, or horseback will discover the remains of shrines and towers, villages and cliff dwellings. Tucked into this majestic setting is the idyllic guest ranch that owners Garry and Ming Adams have lovingly created over the past 10 years. Quaint guest cabins are set among green swaths of pastureland, orchards, and

a meandering stream. The property is also a working farm and ranch, where Ming and Garry are dedicated to raising livestock and growing produce using sustainable methods and adhering to the highest ethical standards. And their devotion to the land and to all the creatures that live on it is apparent to anyone who visits: a sense of peace and contentment felt by both man and beast is pervasive throughout this enchanting location. The guesthouses at Canyon of the Ancients Ranch range from charming restored log cabins to larger Western-style stone or adobe houses. Homey stone fireplaces and rustic furniture combine with an eclectic selection of art and antiques in each of the lodging choices. All are equipped with modern kitchens and baths, and a touch of Ming decor magic. Settle in, and make yourself at home.

35

Canyon of the Ancients Guest Ranch is a working farm, and all of the creatures that live here are treated with care and respect. And they are curious about visitors! The Adams' Black Baldy, Mickey, greets the couple each day as they go about their morning rounds. As the sun comes up at the ranch, Ming will be happy to bring you fresh eggs for breakfast. And don't be surprised if Garry suggests you join him on a climbing or hiking excursion into the canyons to visit ancient ruins and petroglyphs.

Guests from around the world arrive regularly at Canyon of the Ancients Guest Ranch, drawn to the peace and seclusion of this remote luxury lodging. The ranch welcomes visitors year-round. The pastures and orchards are lush and green during the glorious days of spring and summer, and cottonwood trees provide needed shade. In fall and winter the landscape becomes more dramatic. Guests are often invited up to the Adams' home, an adobe encampment (*left*) that sits high up on a rise above the farm, for a cup of tea and some conversation.

Colorado is a land of arid deserts, deep river canyons, and the snow-covered
Rocky Mountains. Much of the state's 66.7 million acres remain wild and untamed.
Catching a glimpse of Colorado's wild inhabitants is likely in any region of the
state, from The Four Corners to The Front Range. Considered by Native Americans
to be the most intelligent of animals, the coyote makes its home in the high mesas
as well as near urban locations. The coyote's haunting call has been heard throughout this land since ancient times. The mountain lion is generally more elusive,
living in the most remote areas of the state. These images were captured at the
Canyon of the Ancients Guest Ranch.

41

Native American Dance Ceremonies can be enjoyed all over Colorado, and The Four Corners region has an especially vibrant Native American tradition.

Ceremonial costumes are infused with symbols of power and protection, and may include star-shaped designs as well as the sun medallion affirming the warrior's identity. Eagle feathers, which a dancer may spend a lifetime collecting, offer strength and protection when facing one's enemies.

The Warrior Dance is a dramatic performance, in which the dancer takes on the persona of the young warrior coming home from battle, recounting his deeds to his admiring onlookers.

Music and storytelling play vital roles in traditional dance ceremonies. A favorite tale concerns a young warrior, a woodpecker, and the origin of the flute.

Many generations ago people had drums, gourds, and bull rattlers, but no flutes.
At that time a young man went out to hunt. He found himself deep in the forest,
where he saw a woodpecker making holes in a branch. When a gust of wind
blew through that branch it made a beautiful sound.

The young man returned to his village. He found a cedar branch,
hollowed it out and whittled it into the shape of a bird with a long neck.
He had made the first flute and it made a lovely, ghost-like sound.

In this village there was a powerful Chief who had a beautiful daughter.
The young man made a special song to play on his flute,
so that she would fall in love with him.

The Chief's daughter heard the sound and she could not resist leaving her father's tipi
and following that haunting sound. In no time she stood next to the young man. She
said, "Young man, I like you! Let your parents send a gift to my father.
No matter how small, it will be accepted. Do it right now!"

The Chief's daughter became the young hunter's wife.
All the other young men began to whittle cedar branches to attract young women.
Thanks to cedar, a woodpecker, the wind, and a young hunter who shot no elk but
knew how to listen, the flute came to be.

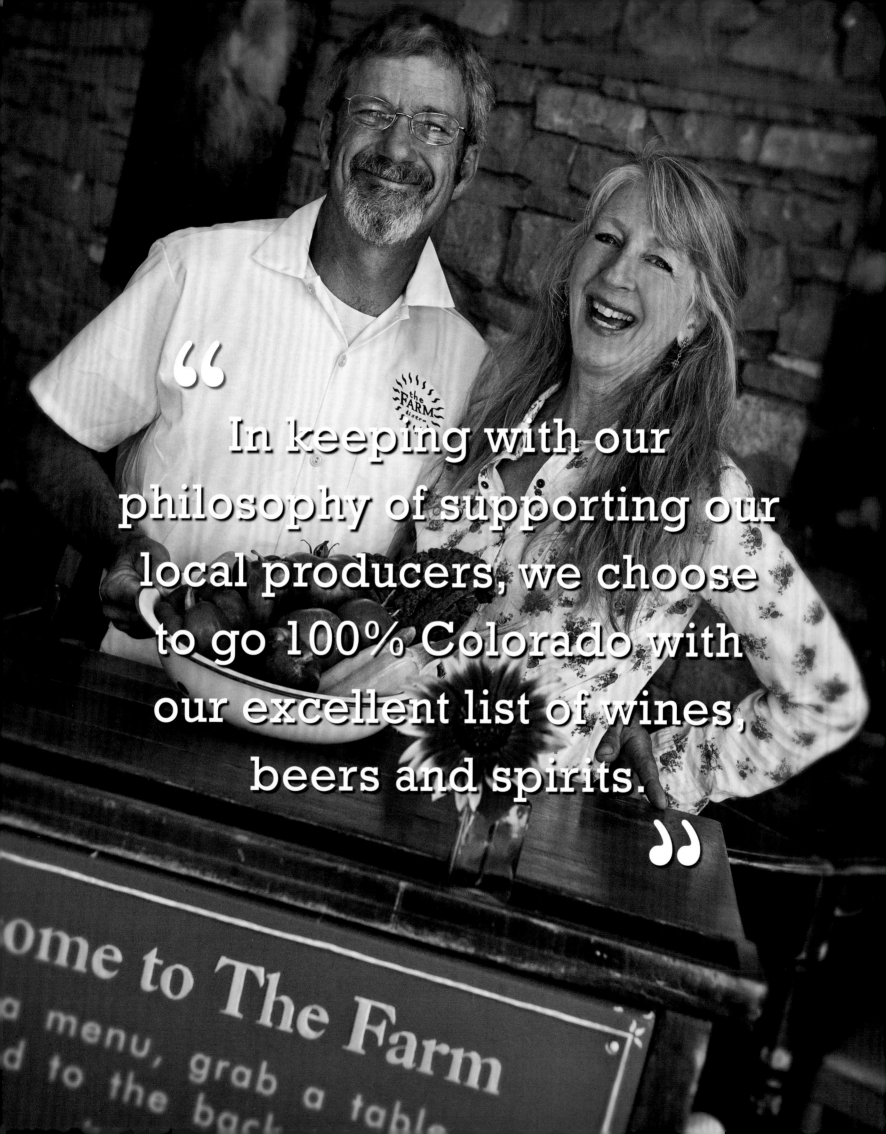

" In keeping with our philosophy of supporting our local producers, we choose to go 100% Colorado with our excellent list of wines, beers and spirits. "

The Farm Bistro

34 West Main Street, Cortez

Partnering with local farmers and ranchers, The Farm Bistro is on a mission to reduce the local community's reliance on food that comes from far away – and in doing so, prove that good, clean food made from scratch is always in demand.

The Farm Bistro is a charming combination of restaurant and community-gathering place located in what was once the old post office on Main Street in Cortez. Diners are welcomed by cheerful farm tables decorated with potted herbs, while a fireplace, comfortable couch and bookshelves, and a friendly bar towards the back of the bistro create a cozy retreat. Owners Rusty and Laurie Hall (*left*) didn't start out with grand aspirations when they first began selling produce from their garden at the local market. But demand for their fresh salads and hearty home cooking encouraged them to open The Farm Bistro in 2009. At that time, Cortez had few options for healthy dining, and The Farm Bistro has been a leader in setting the example for creating dishes that have flavor and nutrition, and are

made from locally sourced ingredients. The Halls work closely with the area's farmers and ranchers to compose a menu based on vegetables, grains, meats and cheeses produced within 75 miles of Cortez. The Farm Bistro's extensive list of wines, beers and spirits is 100 percent Colorado based. While The Farm Bistro's menu changes with the seasons, some of chef Rusty Hall's signature dishes include hearty Moroccan-style lamb meatballs with roasted potatoes and kale, and chicken potpie with a flaky pastry crust made from locally ground wheat. Traditional Native American ingredients such as blue corn flour and Anasazi beans are used in a number of dishes. And farm-fresh salads are always on the menu, with a favorite being the salad of roasted beets and fennel with herbed chevre.

MESA VERDE
NATIONAL PARK
WORLD HERITAGE SITE
MONTEZUMA

Mesa Verde National Park

A World Heritage Site, Mesa Verde National Park sits at an elevation of between 7,000 and 8,500 feet and covers over 50,000 acres. Steep cliffs, deep canyons and narrow trails are characteristic of the spectacular terrain. The park includes nearly 5,000 archeological sites, 600 of which are the famous cliff dwellings of the Ancestral Pueblo people.

Cliff Dwellings

From a distance, the Mesa Verde plateau rises impressively above the desert valley, its lush green, table-like form in stark contrast to the browns and golds of the surrounding landscape.

Mesa Verde was seasonally inhabited beginning around 7,500 BCE, by nomadic hunter-gatherer peoples. Around 1,400 years ago the inhabitants built the first pueblos; by the end of the 12th century the Ancestral Puebloans began to construct the massive cliff dwellings, for which Mesa Verde is known, in the protected alcoves of the canyon walls. These multistory buildings, kivas, and defensive towers could only be reached by a perilous climb from the valley below or equally dizzying descent from the mesa above.

Mysteriously, the cliff settlements were abandoned 75 to 100 years later. Since the late 13th century these painstakingly constructed, starkly beautiful dwellings have remained empty.

Ancient Petroglyphs

Hidden in deep canyons or high above narrow cliffside trails, ancient petroglyph artwork can be discovered throughout The Four Corners region of Colorado. Petroglyphs are images that hold special meaning for the creator, etched on a rock surface. Some say these images were carved by shamans and represent visions seen in a trance. Others believe the petroglyphs record historical events, or leave a map of hunting sites and water sources. Today, the stories behind these ancient rock inscriptions of birds and animals, handprints, and undulating lines can only be guessed at. This petroglyph from Mesa Verde may tell the story of the Mountain Sheep Clan and the Eagle Clan separating from other tribes and returning to their place of origin. The spiral shapes are thought to represent a *sipapu*, a place where the ancient Pueblo people believed they emerged from the earth.

— WEST ELKS —

The West Elks region is located in Delta County, in west-central Colorado, and is known for winding country roads, gorgeous mountain vistas, and high-altitude vineyards. Bounded on the east by the West Elks mountain range, the Grand Mesa to the north, and canyons and high desert to the southwest, the area is informally referred to as The North Fork Valley, for the North Fork of the Gunnison River, which runs through the region's center. Paonia and Hotchkiss are the primary agricultural centers. Compared to other mountainous regions in Colorado, West Elks benefits from relatively mild weather year-round. Early settlers recognized the area as being conducive to agriculture, and fruit trees were planted in the 1880s. By the 1892 World's Fair in Chicago, fruit from the town of Paonia was already winning awards. Cattle and sheep ranchers also moved into the area in the late 19th century, and continue their rugged lifestyle even today. Though Prohibition in the early 20th century forced many early grape growers to pull out their vines, winemaking resumed in 1970s. The climate of West Elks is referred to as semi-arid desert. Winter temperatures average in the low 40s by day, and the low teens at night. Summer highs average in the high 80s during the day, and low 50s at night. Average rainfall is 15.5 inches; average snowfall 47.2 inches. Grapes grown in this region include Riesling, Gewürztraminer, Chardonnay, Pinot Noir, and several hybrid varietals. Both Hotchkiss and Paonia have bustling small towns, with farm-to-table restaurants and a vibrant local arts scene. The West Elks Wilderness is Colorado's fifth largest wilderness tract, with many popular trails for hiking and mountain biking. The North Fork Valley has the highest concentration of organic farms anywhere in Colorado and the concern for low impact, low chemical growing is important to winemakers in the region as well. Winemaker dinners and tastings at individual vineyards are popular with locals and visitors year-round.

{ *The highest altitude vineyards in the northern hemisphere are located in West Elks, one of two designated American Viticultural Areas (AVAs) in the State of Colorado, with the proper characteristics to support the growth of* Vitis vinifera. }

Alfred Eames Cellars

Est. 1994

In the ruggedly beautiful landscape of Paonia, winemakers like Eames Petersen are dedicated to growing Vitis vinifera at high altitude; the results, says Petersen, are wines with more depth and character than those made from grapes grown in more temperate climates.

In 1984, Eames Petersen set to work in Paonia, compelled by a vision of developing wines that would evoke the lush, deep flavors of those varieties he had enjoyed as a young man while living in Spain. Today, Petersen's relaxed, laid-back style belies the talent and devotion that have gone into creating his Tempranillo, Collage, Sangre del Sol, Syrah, and estate-grown Pinot Noir, limited edition wines that are sought after by private clients and restaurants from Denver to Aspen to Chicago.

Owner Alfred Eames Petersen

Winemakers Alfred Eames Petersen and Devin Petersen

Coordinates 38°49'34.3"N 107°36'14.3"W

Altitude 5,980 ft

Annual Rainfall Liquid precipitation 19.3" (14" rain; 53" snow)

Dominant Soil Type Clay loam

Prominent Wines Pinot Noir, Bordeaux-style blends, and Tempranillo

Annual Production 1,500 cases

Wine Tasting Available By appointment and during local events

Notable Awards The cellar's policy is to not submit to wine competitions

Website www.alfredeamescellars.com

Convinced that the grapes grown in Paonia at nearly 6,000 feet were world class, Petersen established Alfred Eames Cellars in 1994. While there are many reasons to plan a visit to Alfred Eames Cellars, the possibility of viewing the decidedly romantic, underground cellar is certainly a good one. Red wines are fermented in open vats, barrel-aged in French Oak, and are unfined and unfiltered. White wines are barrel fermented and lightly filtered. The cellar was constructed by artist Steve Kornher of San Miguel de Allende in Mexico.

Devin Peterson has recently joined his father as partner and winemaker at Alfred Eames Cellars. "Devin was out in the world," said Eames, "and now he's come home." Like many of the next generation of winemakers, Devin – whose name means poet in the original Gaelic – is perfecting his craft while considering opportunities to evolve and develop the winery without losing the sense of intimacy and care that customers have come to cherish. (*This Page*) Petersen samples an estate-grown Pinot Noir, under the serene gaze of West Elks' Mount Lamborn.

Delicious Orchards Organic Farm Market and Café

HOTCHKISS

The North Fork Valley of Colorado is home to this unique family-run enterprise that is as much a community hub as it is a traditional business. Guests are encouraged to relax and stay awhile. Head out to the orchard to pick cherries, pears, peaches, and apples or kick back in the shade with a healthy sandwich and a cool Big B's cider from the café. An old-fashioned rope swing keeps children entertained, and on weekend nights there's often a local musician picking out tunes at the bandstand. Not ready to leave just yet? Delicious Orchards makes it easy to stick around for the night, with a small, tidy camping area tucked in among the orchards. Pitch a tent under the stars, and enjoy sweet dreams among the peach and cherry trees.

63

Leroux Creek Inn & Vineyard

Est. 2000

These secluded acres on the southeast flank of the Grand Mesa provide a gentle refuge from the outside world, where guests, and animals, wild and domestic, all seem to settle into contented harmony.

Shaded by apricot trees, the adobe-style Leroux Creek Inn looks out on a hillside expanse of grapevines that immediately calls to mind the South of France. In 2000, French-born Yvon Gros and his wife Joanna purchased the property and set to work planting the vineyards with sturdy, hybrid varietals. The inn was renovated to create a luxurious southwestern hideaway. During the summer months, dinners hosted by Yvon and Joanna under the property's large outdoor canopy are a highly anticipated event, open to local residents and visitors.

Owners Yvon Gros and Joanna Reckert

Winemaker Yvon Gros

Coordinates 38°50'13.5"N 107°46'46.6"W

Altitude 5,931 ft

Annual Rainfall Liquid precipitation 20.4" (16" rain; 44" snow)

Dominant Soil Type Stony loam

Prominent Wines Red Chambourcin, Cayuga White

Annual Production 500 cases

Wine Tasting Available Yes

Restaurant Breakfast for Inn guests; charcuterie, crudité and gourmet picnic available in the winery

Accommodation 5 guest rooms with private baths

Website www.lerouxcreekvineyards.com

" We love to watch our guests when they arrive at the inn and winery – immediately there is a big sigh of contentment. "

The view from the terrace at Leroux Creek Inn. Visitors might be forgiven for imagining they are in Provence. From the terrace, trails lead to a private creek where all is quiet and serene.

Joanna inspecting the vineyards. In addition to hosting guests at the inn, Joanna has also created a line of handmade skincare items, available to guests, using grapeseed oil and extracts.

Terror Creek Winery

PAONIA

High atop Garvin Mesa the view is breathtaking from Terror Creek Winery, which overlooks the North Fork Valley of the Gunnison River from an elevation of 6,417 feet. Terror Creek is known not only as the highest altitude commercial winery and vineyard in Colorado, but also in the entire northern hemisphere. Joan Mathewson, owner with her husband John, is one of the pioneer winemakers in Colorado. Trained in Switzerland, Joan produces a Dry Riesling for Terror Creek, as well as Gewürztraminer, Chardonnay, Pinot Noir, and a Gamay Noir and Pinot Noir blend – all from Colorado grapes. Perfect for celebrating the high life.

DELTA & MONTROSE

Delta and Montrose counties lie just south of the Grand Valley and west of the West Elks AVA. This wine region is characterized by geographic diversity: Delta county includes the high elevation vineyards of Cedaredge along the flat top of the Grand Mesa, while the lower elevation farmlands and vineyards of Olathe are in Montrose County, further south. The Delta County area was originally home to the Ute Indian people. In 1883, the Colorado legislature created Delta County, named for the city of Delta and the location of the delta of the Uncompahgre River. Visitors traveling to Delta County for winetasting may also want to explore historical sites like Fort Uncompahgre, a reconstruction of an original trading post used by traders, trappers, and Native Americans, and the 200-year-old Ute Council Tree, a designated Colorado Landmark dedicated to the Ute tribe's Chief Ouray and his wife, Chipeta. In summer, Coloradans flock to Montrose County in search of a refreshing glass of local wine and the region's famed Olathe sweet corn. While exploring the region, a side trip not to be missed is a visit to the breathtaking Black Canyon of the Gunnison. Trails wander along the rim of the Canyon, and hikers might want to hold onto something steady when peering over the cliff at the river that lies 2,000 feet below. In the milder farming regions of Delta and Montrose, where temperatures range from a high of 80 to 90 degrees in summer and rarely go below freezing in winter, winemakers grow Cabernet Sauvignon, Merlot, Lemberger, and Chardonnay. Here, beneath the shade of cottonwood trees or seated in an eclectic art-filled tasting room, visitors will be tempted to spend a lazy afternoon sampling some of Colorado's award-winning wines before heading out to pick up local eggs and produce at country farm stands. The climate changes dramatically in high altitude Cedaredge, where winter temperatures can average in the teens and there is significant snowfall. Hybrids are grown here, as well as Pinot Noir and Rieslings. In summertime, a drive along the Grand Mesa Scenic Highway offers stunning views and an escape from the heat of the valley below.

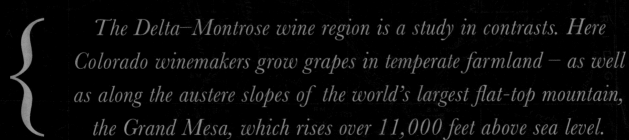

{ The Delta–Montrose wine region is a study in contrasts. Here Colorado winemakers grow grapes in temperate farmland – as well as along the austere slopes of the world's largest flat-top mountain, the Grand Mesa, which rises over 11,000 feet above sea level. }

Crag Crest Cellar
CEDAREDGE

Winemaker David Aschwanden produces wine from grapes grown in the Grand Valley as well as those grown on the slopes of the Grand Mesa in his own high-altitude vineyard at 6,800 feet in Cedaredge (*shown here*). Red wines are extended barrel aged in French oak for at least 30 months, while whites are aged in stainless steel. Varieties include Cabernet Sauvignon, Cabernet Franc, Merlot, and Chardonnay, all from Colorado grapes. Fall 2016 saw the opening of Crag Crest's tasting room and enlarged cellar space on Aschwanden's picturesque farm property, open to the public.

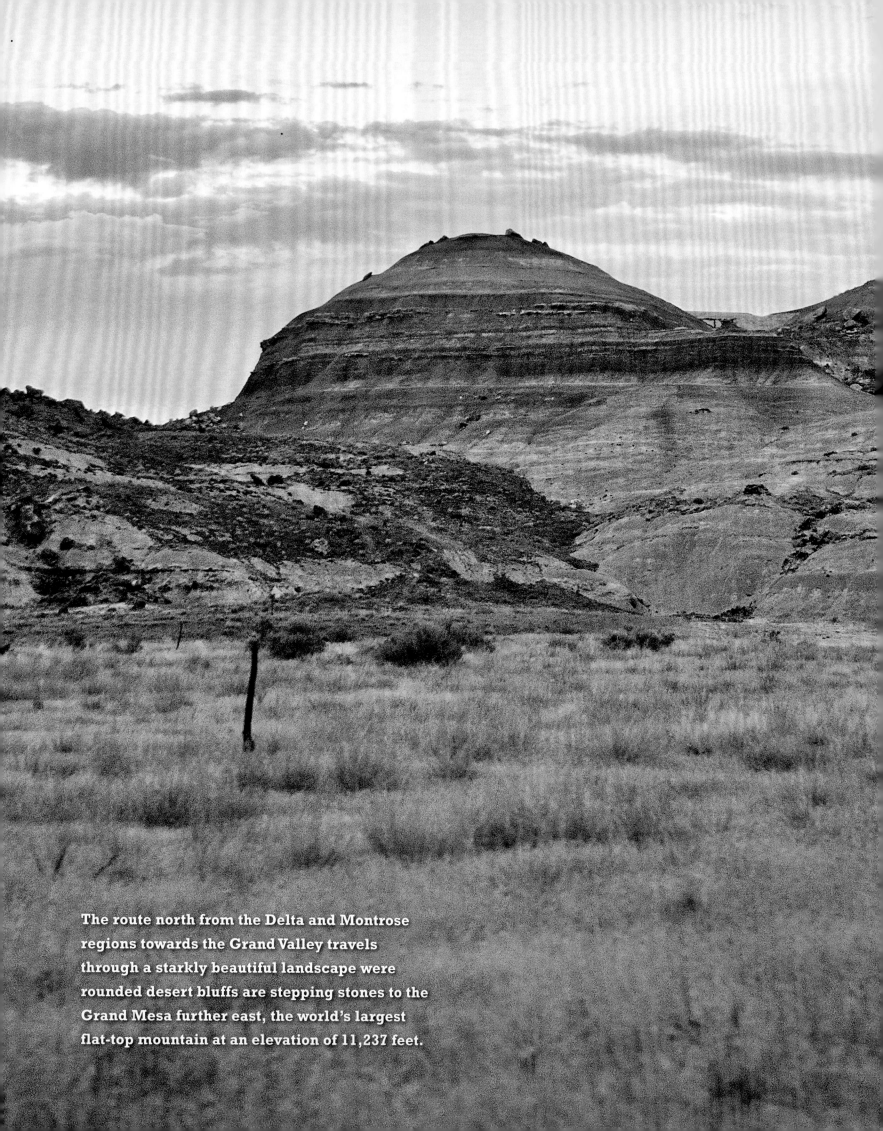

The route north from the Delta and Montrose
regions towards the Grand Valley travels
through a starkly beautiful landscape were
rounded desert bluffs are stepping stones to the
Grand Mesa further east, the world's largest
flat-top mountain at an elevation of 11,237 feet.

80

— GRAND VALLEY —

The mighty Colorado River winds through the Grand Valley, creating a miraculous swath of green and fertile farmland beneath the massive bulk of the Grand Mesa to the south and the austere Book Cliffs to the north. Located in Mesa County, in western Colorado, the Grand Valley American Viticultural Area provides more than 80 percent of Colorado's wine grapes. Here one finds the quirky historic town of Palisade, and country roads that wind through the vineyards and orchards of East Orchard Mesa, the mountain-biking mecca of Fruita, and the bustling university city of Grand Junction, location of a major regional airport. Just west of Grand Junction are the iconic red rock cliffs, spires, and arches of the Colorado National Monument. Hot summer days and cool nights create the perfect climate for growing the noble grapes: Cabernet Sauvignon, Pinot Noir, Merlot, Syrah, Chardonnay, Sauvignon Blanc, and Riesling. Cabernet Franc is another successful grape variety, and growers and winemakers are experimenting with hardy hybrids. In the late 19th century settlers arrived in the valley that had previously been inhabited by the Ute tribes. The region soon became known for its excellent fruit production. Grapes were grown in the valley, but during Prohibition growers were forced to uproot their vines, replacing them with other crops. Interest in the cultivation of *Vitis vinifera* in the Grand Valley was sparked in the late 1960s and early 1970s. Pioneering winemakers began to explore the Grand Valley: Colorado Mountain Vineyards (which would later evolve into Colorado Cellars) produced its first bottle of wine from Colorado grapes in 1978; Plum Creek was founded by Doug Phillips in 1984; Stephen Smith launched Grande River in 1987; and Parker and Mary Carlson opened Carlson Vineyards in 1988. Today, there are over 140 wineries in the state including cideries and meaderies. Discover the heart of Colorado wine country with a tour of lush vineyards and charming downtown tasting rooms along Palisade's Fruit and Wine Byway. A table at one of the valley's farm-to-table restaurants is a perfect way to wind down the day, before settling in to a welcoming inn as your base for further winetasting adventures tomorrow.

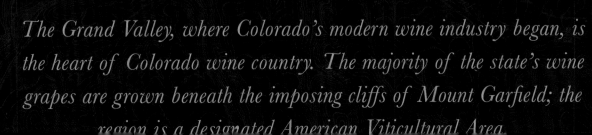

{ *The Grand Valley, where Colorado's modern wine industry began, is the heart of Colorado wine country. The majority of the state's wine grapes are grown beneath the imposing cliffs of Mount Garfield; the region is a designated American Viticultural Area.* }

In the midst of the unrelentingly harsh desert landscape, Palisade is an oasis of green farmlands and vineyards, as seen from the Palisade Rim trail. The Palisade Rim is part of the Grand Mesa, where plans are underway to create a thrilling 33-mile mountain bike descent referred to as The Palisade Plunge. Starting at 10,800 feet elevation, the trail will "plunge" 6,300 feet to the valley floor.

Colorado Cellars

Est. 1978 as Colorado Mountain Vineyards

High up on Palisade's East Orchard Mesa, Colorado Cellars commands a panoramic view of the Book Cliffs, from Mount Garfield to Mount Lincoln. The history of this winery is deeply entwined with the history of Colorado's wine industry itself.

A southwestern-style tasting room opens out onto a patio with views of rolling lawn and picturesque gazebo; bordering the property are vineyards and fields of lavender. If owner Rick Turley is serving wine at the tasting room, visitors may have the opportunity to learn about the growth and development of the state's wine industry, and the important role Colorado Cellars has played in the history of Colorado wine.

Owners Richard and Padte Turley

Winemaker Padte Turley

Viticulturists Rick and Padte Turley

Coordinates 39°04'29.2"N 108°23'41.2"W

Altitude 4,790 ft

Annual Rainfall Liquid precipitation 11.2" (10" rain; 12" snow)

Dominant Soil Type Clay loam

Prominent Wines Cabernet Sauvignon, Syrah, Merlot, Elderberry wine and other Fruit Wines, Spiced Mead

Annual Production 25,000 cases

Wine Tasting Available Year-round

Notable Awards Over 1,000 awards. Of note: winner of the people's choice award at the first annual Colorado Wine Fest in Manitou Springs

Website www.coloradocellars.com

The Turley's have one of the most extensive wine cellars, utilizing cold fermentation with native yeasts, natural fining and filtration, stainless steel fermentation tanks, concrete amphora tanks, 25 hectoliter French oak tanks, and a mixture of American, French, and Hungarian oak barrels for aging and select fermentation. Their overall philosophy is one of emphasizing minimal processing at all stages.

In addition, Colorado Cellars has an extensive collection of library wines, dating back to 1978.

Through its origins as Colorado Mountain Vineyards, established in 1978, Colorado Cellars is the oldest Colorado winery still in operation today. Rick and Padte Turley, active in the industry since the mid-1970s and involved in Colorado Mountain Vineyards in the early days, took full ownership of the winery in 1989. They changed the name to Colorado Cellars and today affirm, "we are proud that Colorado Cellars continues to sell wines made under Colorado Winery License No. 5, the state's oldest license still in existence."

For 40 years Rick, Padte and their family have worked to develop Colorado Cellars into the well-recognized brand it is today. Colorado Cellars offers 27 different wines, including traditional French-style wines such as Cabernet Sauvignon, Merlot, Syrah, Chardonnay, and Pinot Grigio; they also produce a list of refreshing fruit wines and prominent among these are Blackberry Wine, Chokecherry Wine, and Elderberry Wine. Meads and port are also available, and Colorado Cellars is one of the few wineries to produce a Champagne in the traditional manner.

Rick and Padte Turley form the perfect "yin and yang" winemaking team. Gregarious and outgoing, Rick Turley travels throughout the state, promoting his wines to longtime customers. Padte Turley, the more reserved member of the team, is nonetheless one of the most experienced winemakers in Colorado with one of the largest collections of awards to her name, and for her there is nothing better than heading out to the vineyards to nurture, prune, and tend to her next crop.

The Turleys grow grapes and fruit on their property, and keep bees for their honeywine. Natural growing techniques are the rule in the vineyards and orchards: techniques include leaf removal (thinning) and canopy management, reintroduction of grape pumice as fertilizer, minimal natural pest control, measured irrigation application, and gentle hand harvesting.

THE PIONEER OF COLORADO WINES

COLORADO
MOUNTAIN
VINEYARDS

Wines
Champagne
Ports
Fruit Wines

Naturally Grown and Gently Hand Harvested

Rocky Mountain
Vineyards

"Critter"

RoadKill Red
2014
American Semi-Sweet Red Table Wine

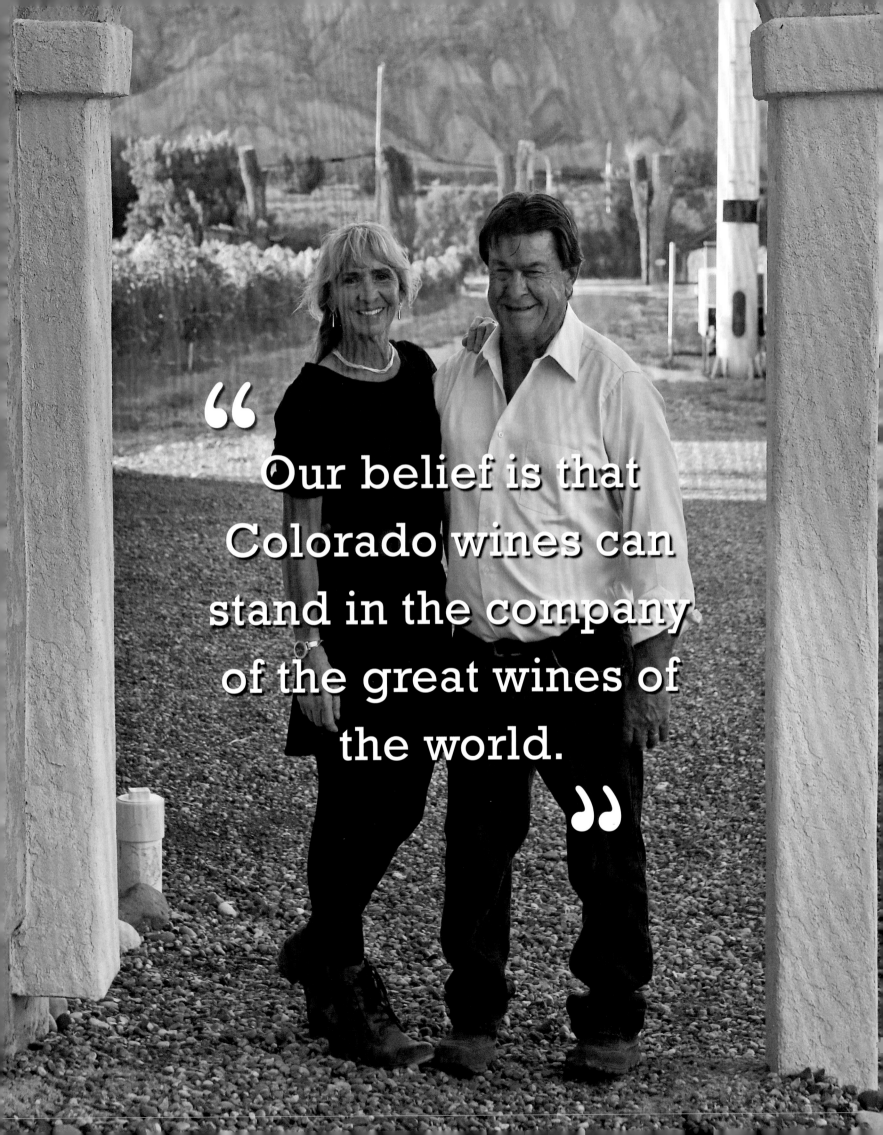

" Our belief is that Colorado wines can stand in the company of the great wines of the world. "

Absolute Prestige Limousine Services

GRAND JUNCTION

Whether you are planning to be full of glamor or full of wine (or both!) your Colorado wine experience can be stylishly completed with a chauffeur-driven ride. Absolute Prestige Limousine Service has been serving the Western Slope of Colorado since 1999 and has an impressive fleet by all standards. A fully stocked, stretch limousine or sleek SUV is at your service for custom winetasting tours throughout the Grand Valley, or luxury transport service from Grand Junction Regional Airport to Aspen, Telluride, Gateway and more. For those with something a little more old-fashioned in mind, take yourself on a little journey to page 164!

Anita's Pantry and Produce

EAST ORCHARD MESA, PALISADE

This country-style farm stand sits beside the Fruit and Wine Byway as it winds its way across the East Orchard Mesa in Palisade. Visitors will find fruit picked fresh from local farms, and a tempting selection of Anita's homey blends of pickles and relishes, olive oil infusions, jams and jellies at this quirky, family-run business. Spend a little time chatting with owner Anita Hix, and you'll quickly realize she's the unofficial expert on local wineries, restaurants and great things to do in Palisade. Follow her suggestions and you can't go wrong. Anita's son, Ben Haver, helps with the heavy lifting when produce is delivered, while granddaughter Aveigha Baughman is a natural-born saleswoman in the making. What about just one more bag of fresh peaches?

Colterris

Est. 2010

"Here one should be able to produce great Bordeaux-styled wines," thought Theresa and Scott High when they first laid eyes on the rugged terroir they would purchase in the Grand Valley. They would call it Colterris, naming it for Colorado and for the land.

Wine professionals for over 30 years, the Highs traveled the world extensively before settling on Palisade as the ideal location for the wines they wanted to grow. With its high altitude, intense sunlight, and deep river canyons, the land reminded them of Mendoza – the great wine-producing region in Argentina. Today Colterris is Colorado's largest estate winery, with vineyard holdings planted throughout 180 acres extending from the mouth of De Beque Canyon to multiple sites on East Orchard Mesa. Careful consideration has gone into matching each vineyard's mesoclimate to grow the very best possible grape varietal for each vineyard location.

Owners Scott and Theresa High

Winemakers Bo Felton and Justin Jannusch

Vineyard Manager Juan Adan

Coordinates 39°05'06.1"N 108°23'42.0"W south of the Colorado River on East Orchard Mesa
39°06'51.4"N 108°19'33.3"W north of the Colorado River at the mouth of De Beque Canyon

Altitude 4,800 ft

Annual Rainfall Liquid precipitation 10.2" (9" rain; 12" snow)

Dominant Soil Type Clay loam

Prominent Wines Cabernet Sauvignon, Malbec, Merlot, Cabernet Franc, Petit Verdot, Chardonnay, Sauvignon Blanc, Coral White Cabernet Sauvignon

Annual Production 17,500 cases

Wine Tasting Available Year-round at Colterris Winery on North River Road; mid-April to October at Colterris at the Overlook on East Orchard Mesa

Restaurant Picnic items

Website www.colterris.com

95

Some 30 years ago when Scott High proposed to Theresa, he promised her a vineyard. The couple married and spent the next 15 years traveling the world, looking for the perfect location. In 1999 they found their dream on East Orchard Mesa in Palisade. With its high elevation, volcanic soil, protection offered by the Grand Mesa, and the Colorado River valley, Palisade held the perfect climate for the type of wines the Highs wanted to produce.

And so began the careful acquisition of vineyard property. In 2010 Colterris released its first vintage. By 2016, Colterris was producing world-class wines from their vineyards and was becoming more widely recognized and appreciated throughout the region.

The challenges of Colorado's terrain means that most wine-makers typically operate as small, boutique ventures. The Highs had other plans. But in order to reach that next level of production they knew they would need to up the ante – increase capacity and engage some of the brightest young winemaking talent in the country.

In 2016, they made significant acquisitions of additional prime vineyards. Situated beneath the dramatic Roan Plateau, at the mouth of De Beque Canyon on the eastern edge of Palisade, these vineyards are widely recognized as some of the best in Colorado. Breezes blowing down De Beque Canyon keep the vineyards up to 10 degrees warmer than properties just a few miles away, greatly reducing the threat of freeze.

In the fall of 2016, two rising star winemakers joined the Colterris team: Bo Felton, winemaker, was raised in Colorado and completed his degree at the University of Colorado at Boulder. Upon graduation, Felton moved to California, landing coveted positions at Duckhorn Wine Company's Goldeneye and Migration Wine Division. Felton also spent time in New Zealand, working with Rapaura Vintners. Justin Jannusch, assistant winemaker, is also a graduate of the University of Colorado at Boulder and a 10-year veteran winemaker with Colorado's Bookcliff Vineyards. Both of these talented individuals have the knowledge and experience necessary to make exceptional wines "from the Colorado land" and fulfill the vision of Colterris.

"There is a sense of excitement for our entire family these days, as years of hard work and planning at Colterris come to fruition."

A must-stop on the Fruit and Wine Byway is Colterris at the Overlook tasting room on East Orchard Mesa. Visitors can stroll among the lavender gardens and the Highs' collection of outdoor sculpture; wander down a gravel lane between rows of peach trees; rest in the shade of an elegant pavilion high above the farmlands of Palisade and the mighty Colorado River.

The busy outdoor tasting room serves the most popular Colterris varietals, including the Colterris White Cabernet Sauvignon, a refreshing, bright-coral tinted wine made from Cabernet Sauvignon grapes. Light snacks are also served. Next door, cherries and peaches in season can be purchased at the High Country Orchards country store, as well as old-fashioned farm life memorabilia.

(Opposite) Bo Felton in the barrel cave enjoying his new role as winemaker at Colterris. Felton, who had been winemaker at California's Migration Winery, joined Colterris in the fall of 2016.

"One of the cool things about wine, besides drinking it, is the people you drink it with. So drink the wine!"

At the highest irrigated elevation on East Orchard Mesa, Scott High has planted special clones of Malbec. Adjacent to this hilltop vineyard is a unique circle of stones arranged around a bonfire pit, where most certainly Scott has come from time to time to enjoy and appreciate his vineyards – leading Theresa to jokingly refer to the location as "Scott-henge."

Scott High's collection of antique cork screws and wine tools numbers more than 6,000 pieces. Many date back to the early 18th century. Plans are underway to create an on-site gallery of the collection's highlights that will take a visitor through the history of the world of wine.

Situated beneath the dramatic Roan Plateau, at the mouth of De Beque Canyon on the eastern edge of Palisade, these prime vineyards are widely recognized as some of the best in Colorado.

" Running a restaurant is a team sport, and I love what this team has created for the community. "

Bin 707 Foodbar

225 North 5th Street, No. 105, Grand Junction

This hipster favorite in downtown Grand Junction blends mod industrial decor and a stylish bar scene with soul-satisfying American cuisine served at big, family-style farm tables.

Located at the junction of the Colorado and Gunnison rivers, Grand Junction sits in a fertile valley surrounded by red rock bluffs and desert landscape. A lovely historic district boasts tree-lined streets and neighborhood parks surrounded by elegant Victorian homes. Within walking distance is Grand Junction's downtown; here visitors can stroll along shady sidewalks decorated with outdoor sculptures, stopping to enjoy lunch at a casual café – or an impromptu performance by local musicians. An eclectic and growing dining scene is attracting more and more visitors to this Western-style downtown. In the heart of downtown Grand Junction, Bin 707 Foodbar, created by chef Josh Niernberg and his wife Jodi, is a magnet for foodies from across the state. A chef, sommelier, and an industrial designer to boot, Josh has put

together a culinary experience that draws on the best local meats, cheeses and produce from the Grand Valley and the West Elks regions and serves them up in innovative, sometimes unexpected ways. Bin 707 has been so successful at putting Colorado cuisine on the map that Josh has traveled to Mexico, Austin, and recently Chicago as a culinary ambassador on behalf of the State of Colorado. Is life for Josh just one big food party? Maybe. Making Grand Junction even more attractive as a culinary destination, the energetic Josh is launching two new ventures. Taco Party is a quick serve taco shop, with a constantly evolving Colorado-sourced menu and a full-service bar. The fun continues right next door with Dinner Party, a private event space where Josh will host chef and winemaker dinners and experiment with new dining concepts.

What's fresh, local and in season dictates the menu at Bin 707 Foodbar. Blistered banana peppers are served with a sprinkling of fresh ricotta and rosemary agave; multicolored heirloom tomatoes are tossed with Palisade's famed peaches. And Josh's signature soft-boiled egg turns up in the most unlikely places, adding a burst of color, flavor and texture.

The Bin 707 ethos naturally extends to their remarkable cocktail offerings. Bartender Gavin Bistodeau (left) and the Bin 707 team are passionate about creating their magic with local spirits. Farm-fresh ingredients, crisp snow-melt water and bucket-loads of passion have culminated in a rapidly growing movement of more than 50 local distilleries, producing everything from vodka, gin and whiskey to rum, brandy and absinthe. Here, bitters, tinctures, shrubs, infusions, syrups, gastriques and many other ingredients are house-made. No small undertaking but as they say, "the juice is worth the squeeze!"

Colorado Mountain Winefest

Presented by Colorado Association for Viticulture and Enology

Colorado's premier winetasting event is a multiday celebration in the Grand Valley that takes place each year in September. Fall is showtime for Colorado's winemakers and Colorado Mountain Winefest celebrates this season of harvest and hard work. In 2016 the festival, which is organized each year by the Colorado Association for Viticulture and Enology (CAVE), marked its 25th anniversary. Founded in 1987, CAVE was originally known as the Rocky Mountain Association of Vintners and Viticulturalists. In 2010, the organization changed its name to reflect its support of wineries across the entire state. CAVE has been instrumental in giving a voice to Colorado's growing wine industry, and also counts among its members Colorado producers of meads and ciders. Highlights of Colorado Mountain Winefest include winemaker dinners hosted by prominent wineries in their tasting rooms or outdoors in their vineyards; Wine, Dine, and Paint (*this page*) is a whimsical evening of creativity and wine drinking, led by the festival's featured commemorative Winefest poster artist.

CAVE

Cassidee Shull (*opposite page*), Executive Director of CAVE, organizes the annual Colorado Mountain Winefest, which is the largest of its kind in the state. Shull's energy and enthusiasm have been a major force driving awareness of Colorado's growing wine industry, and promoting education and the exchange of ideas among winemakers. More than 50 wineries from across the state participate in Winefest each year, and restaurants throughout the Grand Valley host a variety of food and wine pairing events. Scenic bus tours give visitors a chance to fully immerse themselves in the beauty of the Grand Valley AVA, and also introduce them to Colorado's second AVA, the West Elks region, as well as to the high-altitude vineyards of Cedaredge. The main event is the Festival in the Park, a full-day outdoor celebration featuring grape stomping, live music, seminars, and unlimited pours.

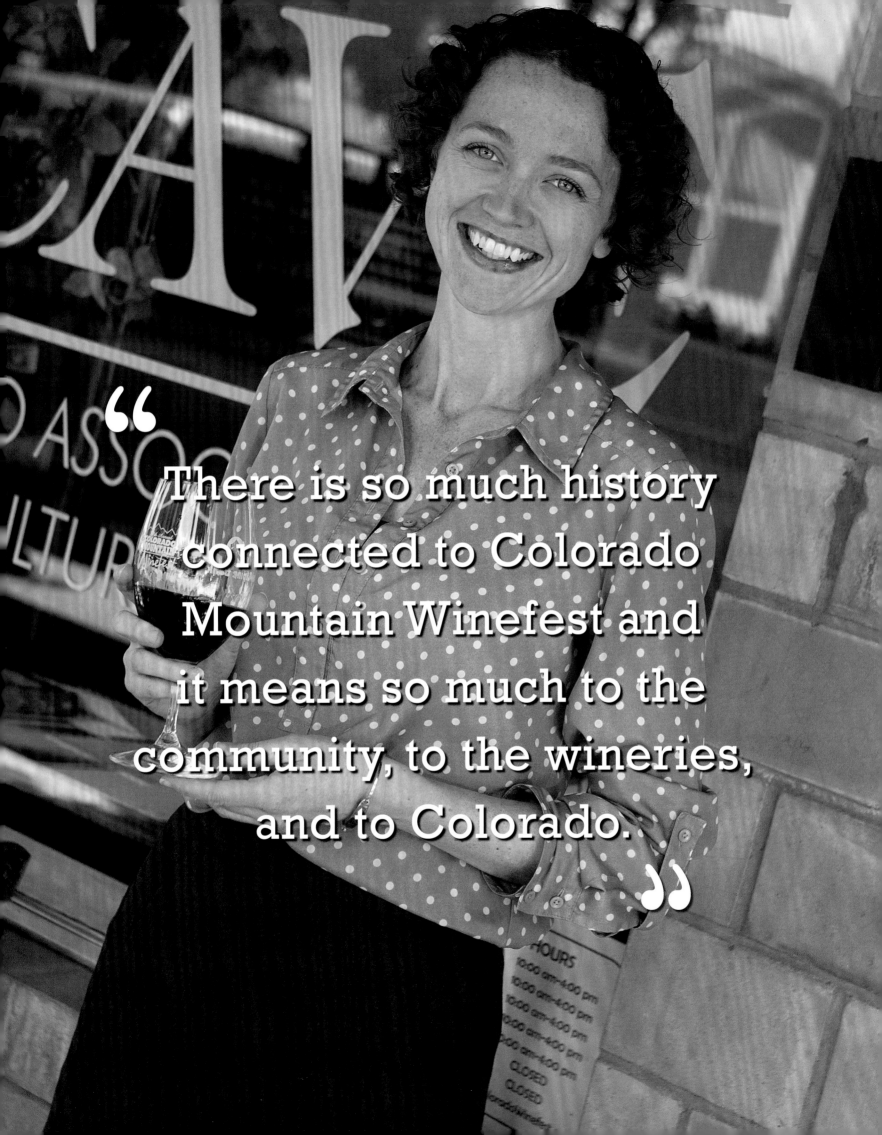

" There is so much history connected to Colorado Mountain Winefest and it means so much to the community, to the wineries, and to Colorado. "

Grande River Vineyards

Est. 1990

One is welcomed into the verdant farmlands of Palisade by the unmistakable sweeping view of Grande River Vineyards. The beautiful, mission-style tasting room surrounded by grapevines immediately announces to the visitor: 'Here is Wine Country.'

Below the majestic Book Cliff mountain range lies Grande River Vineyards. This award-winning winery, one of the oldest in the State of Colorado, is often the first stop for a wine tour on the Fruit and Wine Byway. Founded by Colorado wine pioneer Stephen Smith, who began planting vines in Palisade in 1987, Grande River opened officially in 1990. Today Grande River Vineyards is owned and operated by Stephen Smith and Naomi Shepherd-Smith.

Owners Stephen Smith and Naomi Shepherd-Smith

Winemaker and Vineyard Manager Rainer Thoma

Coordinates 39°07'04.7"N 108°21'43.8"W

Altitude 4,728 ft

Annual Rainfall Liquid precipitation 11.2" (10" rain; 12" snow)

Dominant Soil Type Sandy loam

Prominent Wines Meritage (red and white), Malbec, Syrah, Cabernet Franc, Petit Verdot, Sauvignon Blanc, Viognier, Chardonnay. Dessert wines: Port and Late Harvest Viognier.

Annual Production 5,000 to 7,000 cases

Wine Tasting Available Year-round, 7 days a week except Thanksgiving, Christmas and New Year's Day

Notable Awards Since Grande River's inception the winery has won over 500 awards nationwide

Website www.granderivervineyards.com

115

In 1980, while still working in the oil and gas business, Stephen Smith moved from Wyoming to Denver. Once in Colorado, he fell in with other like-minded businessmen who were becoming interested in reestablishing the Colorado wine industry – and in taking it to the next level.

Smith anticipated a reemergence of the wine business in the Grand Valley. Between 1987 and 1988 he planted 65,000 vines, and Grande River Vineyards' first wines were fermented in 1990. For the next 20 years Grande River was the biggest supplier of grapes in Colorado, and supplied grapes to eight other states. By 2006, grape cultivation was firmly established in the Grand Valley and Smith and Shepherd-Smith decided to sell much of their acreage to local growers from whom they now purchase fruit.

Naomi Shepherd-Smith came from a background in fine arts and non-profit management, and was Executive Director of the Grand Junction Symphony and Musical Arts Association. In 1998 she left this position to move full time into promoting Grande River Vineyards, and to establishing its role as a major force for good within the community.

When Naomi first launched her concert series, *Hear It Through The Grapevine*, the concept of a big, outdoor, community musical event was relatively new. As time went on, other businesses in the Grand Valley jumped on board with their own food, wine or musical affair, widening the range of events offered within the community.

Now, when summer rolls around to the Grand Valley, the great lawn outside Grande River Vineyards becomes the scene of highly anticipated *Hear It Through The Grapevine* concerts, presented on multiple evenings spring through fall. Most concerts raise funds to benefit local charities, all bring together local businesses, residents, and visitors to enjoy the shared pleasures of good friends, good music – and of course – good wine.

Naomi (right) *blends her knowledge and love of wine with a natural ability to organize community events and bring people together.*

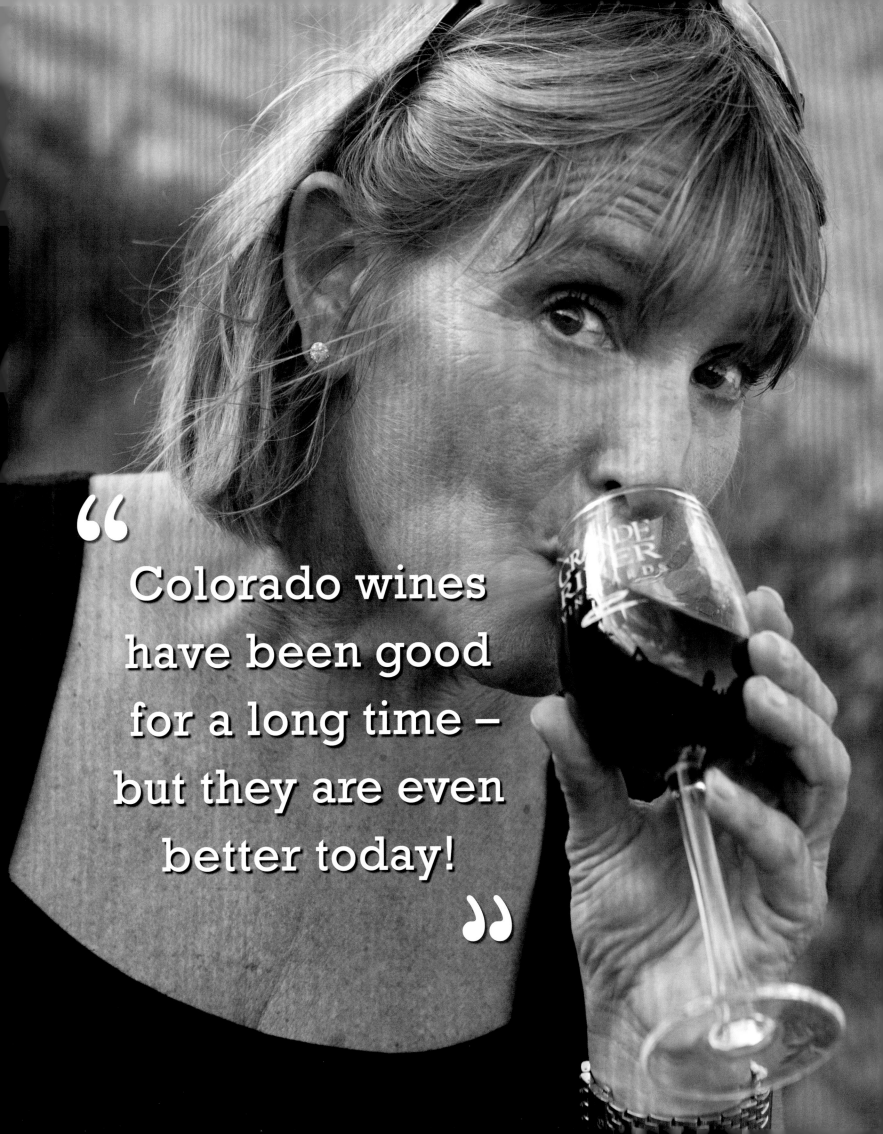

"Colorado wines have been good for a long time – but they are even better today!"

Ten acres of the original Grande River Vineyards still remain under Stephen Smith's (right) and Naomi's ownership, from which they produce Merlot and Petite Verdot. Grande River Vineyards bottles between 5,000 and 7,000 cases of wine per year. All wine is made from 100% Colorado-grown grapes from the Grand Valley.

Grande River's extensive production facilities have allowed the winery to form a cooperative partnership with nearby Wine Country Inn. The winery farms and produces wine for the Inn under a private label.

Education about wine growing and wine enjoyment is important to Naomi, who studied Viticulture, Enology and Wine Marketing at UC Davis. She has created the only "demonstration vineyard" in the Grand Valley, which includes a self-guided tour through nine rows of vines, representing each of the original varieties planted in the vineyards: Sauvignon Blanc, Sémillon, Chardonnay, Viognier, Syrah, Cabernet Sauvignon, Cabernet Franc, Merlot, and Petite Verdot.

Hear It Through The Grapevine, Naomi's inspired summer concert series, encourages the community to kick back with a glass of wine and enjoy the music.

Grande River Vineyards is a top destination for special events. The winery hosts casual wine club members' get-togethers as well as elegant wine dinners and corporate events. Guests are treated to award-winning wines paired with chef-prepared gourmet treats.

Chef Jill Peters is a favorite in the Grand Valley. Peters grew up in the wine business, attended Colorado Mountain Culinary Institute, and began her career working for chefs in Colorado's resort towns. Eventually, she came home to the Grand Valley. Working hand-in-hand with farmers, ranchers and winemakers, Peters has developed a deep respect for the importance of where and how food is grown and the quality of the energy that is devoted to producing it. Chef Peters specializes in preparing nourishing, locally sourced delicacies served at many winemaker dinners and special events in Palisade and Grand Junction. Plants and Bones is Chef Peters' line of organic, homemade bone broths.

Pictured at right, Peters prepares appetizers for a private wine and music event.

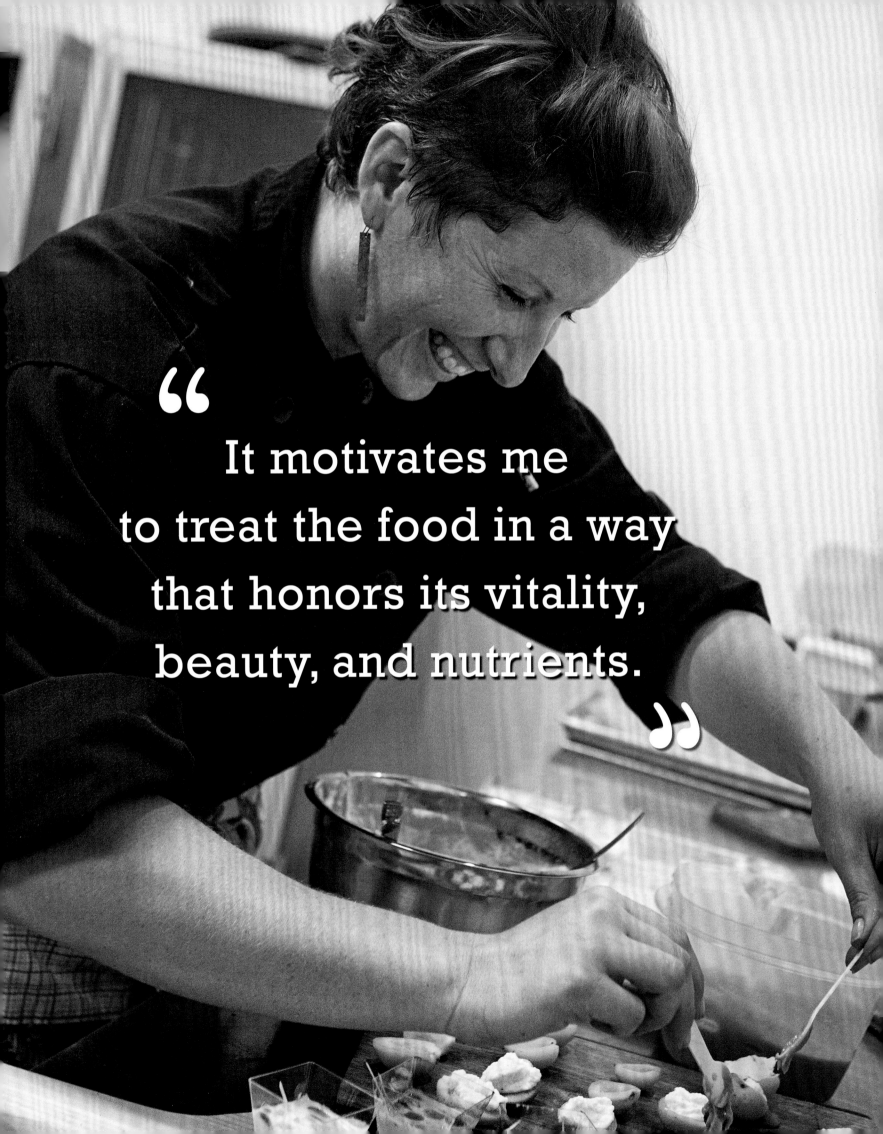

" It motivates me to treat the food in a way that honors its vitality, beauty, and nutrients. "

124

Blaine's Tomatoes
and Farm
CLIFTON

Blaine Diffendaffer's day starts early on
the farm. There are the tomatoes, which
have made Blaine a local celebrity, and
also the cucumbers in the greenhouses to
be tended to. Out in the field, artichokes,
okra, peppers, potatoes, or melons may
be coming into season. Started in 2005 as
a small operation that sold salad greens
to local restaurants, today Blaine's Farm
grows produce that is sought after locally
and across the state.

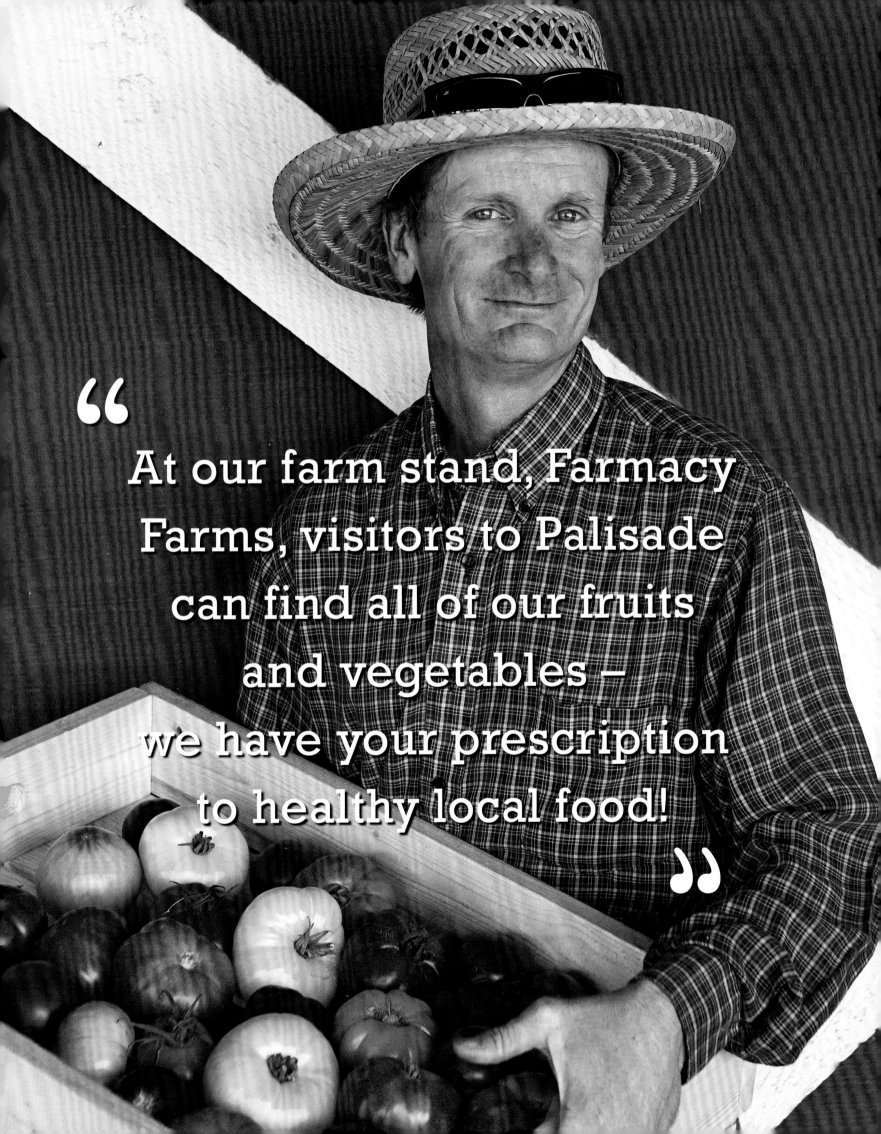

"At our farm stand, Farmacy Farms, visitors to Palisade can find all of our fruits and vegetables – we have your prescription to healthy local food!"

Plum Creek Winery

Est. 1984

For winery owner Sue Phillips, Plum Creek is home. And that feeling of home is beautifully expressed by Plum Creek Winery's downtown tasting room – through its comfortable decor, original artwork, and welcome offering of Colorado's finest wines.

Tucked in beneath the shade of aspens and evergreens, Plum Creek Winery's tasting room is a classic, craftsman-style building located among the farmlands of Palisade. A life-sized sculpture of a stallion by local artist Lyle Nichols adds spirited Western flair to the tasting room's entryway, and lush vineyards surround the property. Plum Creek is one of Colorado's oldest wineries, operating and producing wines under License Number 10, and the extensive property holdings include vineyards in the Grand Valley, as well as Paonia, in the neighboring AVA of West Elks.

Owner Sue Phillips

Winemaker Corey Norsworthy; through 2015, Jenne Baldwin-Eaton

Viticulturist Galen Wallace

Coordinates 39°06'26.0"N 108°21'58.1"W

Altitude 4,500 ft Grand Valley; 6,000 ft West Elks

Annual Rainfall Liquid precipitation 10.2" (9" rain; 12" snow)

Dominant Soil Type Sandy loam

Prominent Wines Grand Mesa Reserve Red, Reserve Chardonnay, Palisade Red, Sauvignon Blanc, Palisade Festival (blend), Cabernet Franc, Dry Riesling

Annual Production 13,000 cases

Wine Tasting Available Year-round, 7 days a week except Thanksgiving, Christmas and New Year's Day

Notable Awards First gold medal at an international wine competition was won at the 1989 San Francisco Fair; since then, numerous national and international awards

Website www.plumcreekwinery.com

Sue Phillips is proud of the winery that she and her late husband Doug established and worked for years to grow into the award-winning brand it is today. At the time Plum Creek was founded in 1984, it was a unique and pioneering notion that one could create premium wines from only those grapes grown in Colorado. But the Phillipses were determined: if there was a bad winter, or a late frost, they would not go in search of grapes from out of state. They would take the hit; they would work harder. Today, the winery produces over 13,000 cases and is one of the most recognized names in Colorado. After her husband's death in 2008 Sue has continued to own and operate Plum Creek Winery. While she recognizes the challenges of producing wine in Colorado's harsh terroir, Sue also reflects that the high altitude and hot sunny days are uniquely favorable conditions that, with a little magic, luck, and artistry, can produce outstanding wines unlike any others.

Plum Creek's vineyard in Paonia (*shown here*), takes high-altitude winemaking to a whole different level. Here, at over 6,000 feet, the wine lover may feel their spirits soar as they look out over the West Elk Mountains – and the thriving vineyard of Chardonnay, Sauvignon Blanc, Pinot Gris, and Riesling.

Lyle Nichols

Artist Lyle Nichols is an eccentric and well-loved figure in the Grand Valley. Each morning, he exits his home in a converted barn via a spiral slide created from an old silo and gets to work on his latest creation. Some of his favorite materials are rusted scraps that remind him of red sandstone or rocks collected from riverbeds in Aspen or Telluride. Nichols' dynamic, life-sized horse sculptures, made from metal scraps, are owned by collectors such as John Hendricks, founder of the Discovery Channel, and Sue Phillips, owner of Plum Creek Winery in Palisade. His simple, elegant spoons and bowls carved from river rocks have appeared in *Architectural Digest*. Nichols' philosophy might be summed up by the sign that hangs above his workshop, a piece of scrap metal from a Joy Compressor that reads, simply: JOY.

PLEASE
STAY ON
OUTSIDE
OF FENCE

REDNECK
FANTASY

Red Fox Cellars

Est. 2012

Nothing Ventured Nothing Gained is the motto of this creative new winery, where Merlot is aged in bourbon barrels and fruit wine cocktails are sipped with a straw on the outside deck.

Operating out of a big, converted office building and warehouse just west of downtown Palisade, Red Fox Cellars is the uninhibited new-kid-on-the-block on the Grand Valley wine scene. Scott and Sherrie Hamilton refer to their wines as "bold and adventurous – respectful but unbound by tradition". Their winery, Red Fox Cellars, is all about experimenting with non-traditional forms of wine production – and wine enjoyment. A sliding garage door pulls open, allowing the indoor tasting room to expand out onto a shady deck where visitors can relax with a glass of wine beneath the majestic Book Cliffs, with an amazing view of Mount Garfield.

Owners Scott and Sherrie Hamilton

Winemaker Chad Hamilton

Viticulturist Scott Hamilton

Coordinates 39°06'16.9"N 108°23'10.0"W

Altitude 4,728 ft

Annual Rainfall Liquid precipitation 10.2" (9" rain; 12" snow)

Dominant Soil Type Crushed granite

Prominent Wines Bourbon Barrel Aged Merlot, 44 Red Blend, Long Day Rosé, Rye Whiskey Barrel Aged Cabernet Franc, Tequila Barrel Aged Chardonnay, Pete's Garage – Cherry Wine, Freestone – Peach Wine, and 8 different Hard Ciders and Perries (Pear Cider) on tap

Annual Production 2,000 cases

Wine Tasting Available Yes

Notable Awards 2015 Long Day Rosé – Double Gold Mesa County Fair. Gold - Governor's Cup & Selected to the Governor's Cup Case 2016

Website www.redfoxcellars.com

Red Fox Cellars is one of the more laid-back stops on the Fruit and Wine Byway. The cozy tasting room with its old barn wood paneling also functions as a gallery showcasing local artists. The outdoor porch is a favorite meeting spot and on balmy summer evenings, food trucks will pull into the big parking area, creating an instant party at the winery.

Winemaker Chad Hamilton (far left) brings a brewing background to his work styling Red Fox's innovative wines, which include Mayan Pirate – a chocolate chili port aged in a rum barrel. Chad's wife Kelly (below left) runs Red Fox's much followed social media.

Enjoying the freedom of moving between the classical and the inventive, owners Scott and Sherrie Hamilton (near left) happily describe themselves as new age students of winemaking.

Scott and Sherrie Hamilton had just moved to Palisade and planted their first crop of vines when the area was hit by record frosts two winters in a row, killing most of their plants. Many people who had invested all of their savings in such a venture would have quit. Somehow, adversity seems to have made the couple more resilient, philosophical, and more open to experimentation and collaboration.

The Hamiltons had sold their ranch and their Denver engineering business in 2011, and moved to Palisade with sons Chad, Kyle, and Erik and Chad's wife Kelly. Neither Scott nor Sherrie had any formal background in winemaking. But what they did have was a capacity for risk taking, an eagerness to learn from other wine professionals, and a belief in their own vision of creating wines that embrace both the traditional and the inventive.

Despite the losses to weather in 2013 and 2014, the Hamiltons' tasting room opened in the fall of 2014, and their first releases were the now widely celebrated Bourbon Barrel Merlot, and the 44 Red Blend. Their eldest son Chad, with a background in brewing, took over as winemaker and in the past several years Red Fox Cellars has become ever more imaginative – aging classic French-style wines in bourbon, rum or tequila barrels, and branching out into fruit wines and hard ciders.

After two years of devastating losses in the vineyard, Scott Hamilton decided to experiment with some of the sturdier American hybrid wine grape varietals. The hybrid St. Vincent grapes (*left*), which grow in a vineyard that surrounds the Hamiltons' home, produce wine with a medium body and bright, fruity taste. Top wire training creates a canopy and supports the St. Vincent grapevine's downward growth pattern. The Colorado Association for Viticulture and Enology (CAVE) recognized Red Fox Cellars as the 2016 Colorado Winery of the Year, a fine testament to years of hard work and vision.

Kyle Hamilton (right) *is the winery's ever-busy jack-of-all-trades, while his dog, the ever-wagging Rusty, is the wine cellar's enthusiastic mascot.*

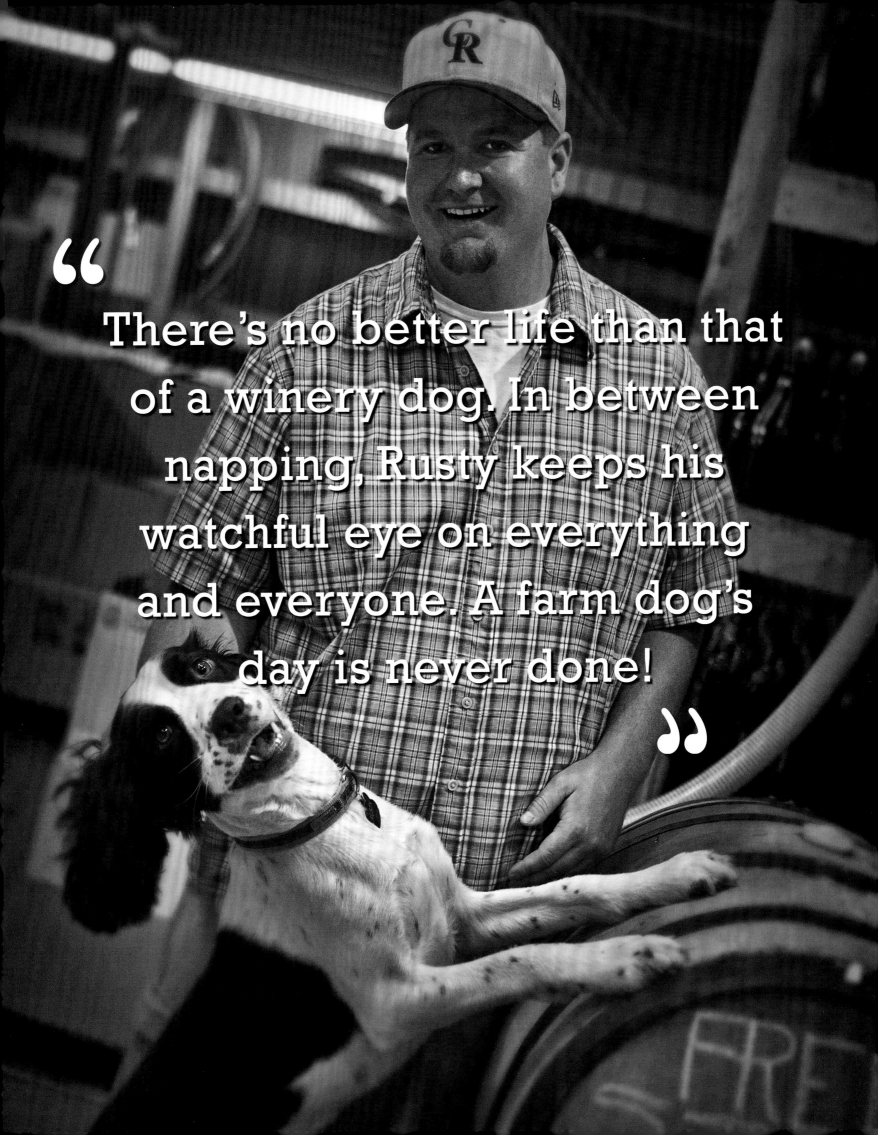

"There's no better life than that of a winery dog. In between napping, Rusty keeps his watchful eye on everything and everyone. A farm dog's day is never done!"

The Palisade Café 11.0

113 West 3rd Street, Palisade

Spanish and Peruvian influences transform a bounty of local meats, cheeses, fruits and vegetables into dishes that are both down-home comforting and excitingly original at this friendly mainstay restaurant in Palisade's town center.

A walk through downtown Palisade is like a walk down memory lane; here, life seems just a little less complicated and hectic. Neighbors greet each other with a friendly wave and hello. Visitors are warmly welcomed by the eclectic mix of business people and farmers, artists and foodies, rafters and bike enthusiasts – all of whom make Palisade their home. And on any given day, it's a good bet that a local festival or farmers market will be in full swing. Guests to Palisade Café 11.0 are likely to be greeted at the door by owner and local Palisade personality John Sabal. If he happens to miss your arrival, you can be sure he'll swing around during your meal to make sure all is well. Sabal, who originally hails from New York City, earned his

restaurant chops working at some of the top resort restaurants in Colorado. His love of food and wine led him inevitably to the Grand Valley. Co-owner Marisol Montoya was also drawn to the area by the lure of fresh, wholesome produce. While Sabal's heritage harkens back to Spain, Montoya grew up in a Peruvian household. Together, they've combined their love of fresh, healthy food with a style that is, in their words, "slightly whimsical and maximum fresh". Begin your day with cinnamon swirl French toast or tortilla Espanola; stop by at midday for a "BLP" – bacon, lettuce, and Palisade peaches – and enjoy a bottle of Colorado wine with a dinner of roast pork belly or grilled Argentinian red shrimp.

143

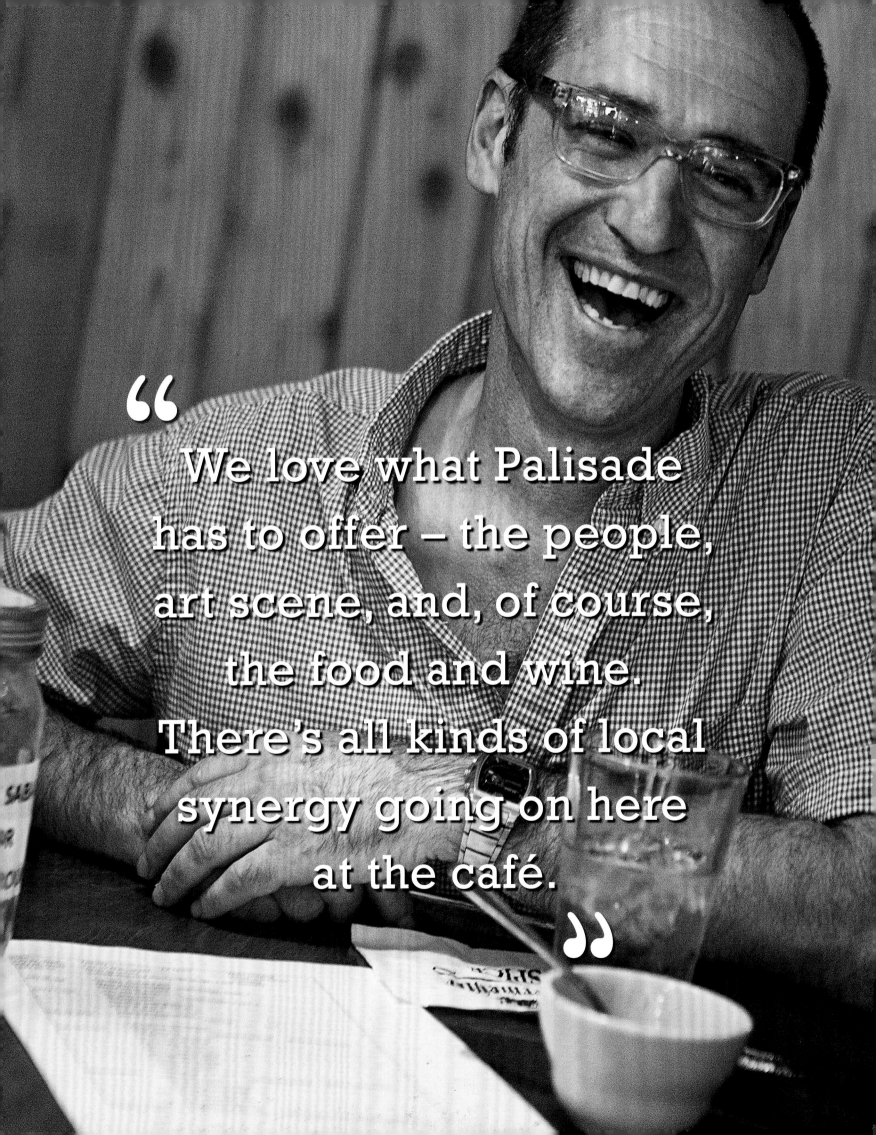

" We love what Palisade has to offer – the people, art scene, and, of course, the food and wine. There's all kinds of local synergy going on here at the café. "

Talbott Farms

EAST ORCHARD MESA

The Talbott family traces its Grand Valley farming roots back to 1907, when their first ancestors arrived. Many of the orchards that today grow peaches, pears, or apples were planted by the pioneering first generation in the Talbott lineage. Today the fifth generation of the family oversees the largest peach production in the State of Colorado, with over 30 varieties of peaches harvested each year. Talbott Farms is also one of the major suppliers of wine grapes, viniferous and hybrids, to many of Colorado's winemakers and the family has launched a line of hard ciders to complement the fresh sweet cider they produce from the region's apple orchards.

Two Rivers Winery and Chateau

GRAND JUNCTION

Established in 1999 by Robert G. Witham, today Two Rivers Winery offers selections produced by winemaker Brandon G. Witham, including Cabernet Sauvignon, Chardonnay, Merlot, Syrah, Riesling, Vintner's Blend, and a Ruby Port. Two Rivers Winery is the proud recipient of over 23 gold medals in international competitions. Tastings are available daily in two elegant tasting rooms, and a country-style inn offers on-site accommodation. The winery's dramatic location beneath the Colorado National Monument makes it a popular stop for winetasting and a busy venue for weddings and other events.

Two Rivers Winery and Chateau is one of the founding members of the Grand Valley Winery Association, a group of seven wineries in the Grand Valley AVA that was formed in 2002 to promote an awareness and appreciation of this important wine-producing region. Most of Colorado's grapes are grown in the Grand Valley, and the region's vineyards are of vital importance to winemakers throughout the state.

The Grand Valley Winery Association spearheads a number of popular winetasting events throughout the year, including Wine into Winter, and Barrel into Spring.

In addition to Two Rivers Winery, members of the Grand Valley Winery Association include (*on the following pages*) Graystone Winery, Carlson Vineyards, DeBeque Canyon Winery, and Garfield Estates. Grande River Vineyards and Plum Creek Winery, also featured in this book, are members of the association as well.

149

Graystone Winery

CLIFTON

This boutique winery, with its signature purple door, was established in 2000. Winner of numerous international competitions for its ruby red and white ports, the Tuscan-style tasting room is open daily.

Carlson Vineyards
EAST ORCHARD MESA, PALISADE
Established in 1988 and one of
the state's oldest wineries.
Winemaker Garrett Portra and
his wife, Cailin, took over in 2015
and today delight customers with
innovative new offerings as well as
traditional favorites.

DeBeque Canyon Winery

DOWNTOWN PALISADE

Owner Bennett Price is one of Colorado's pioneer viticulturists and winemakers. Together with his wife, Davy, Bennett produces a number of traditional varieties. The cozy tasting room is located near the western entrance of De Beque Canyon.

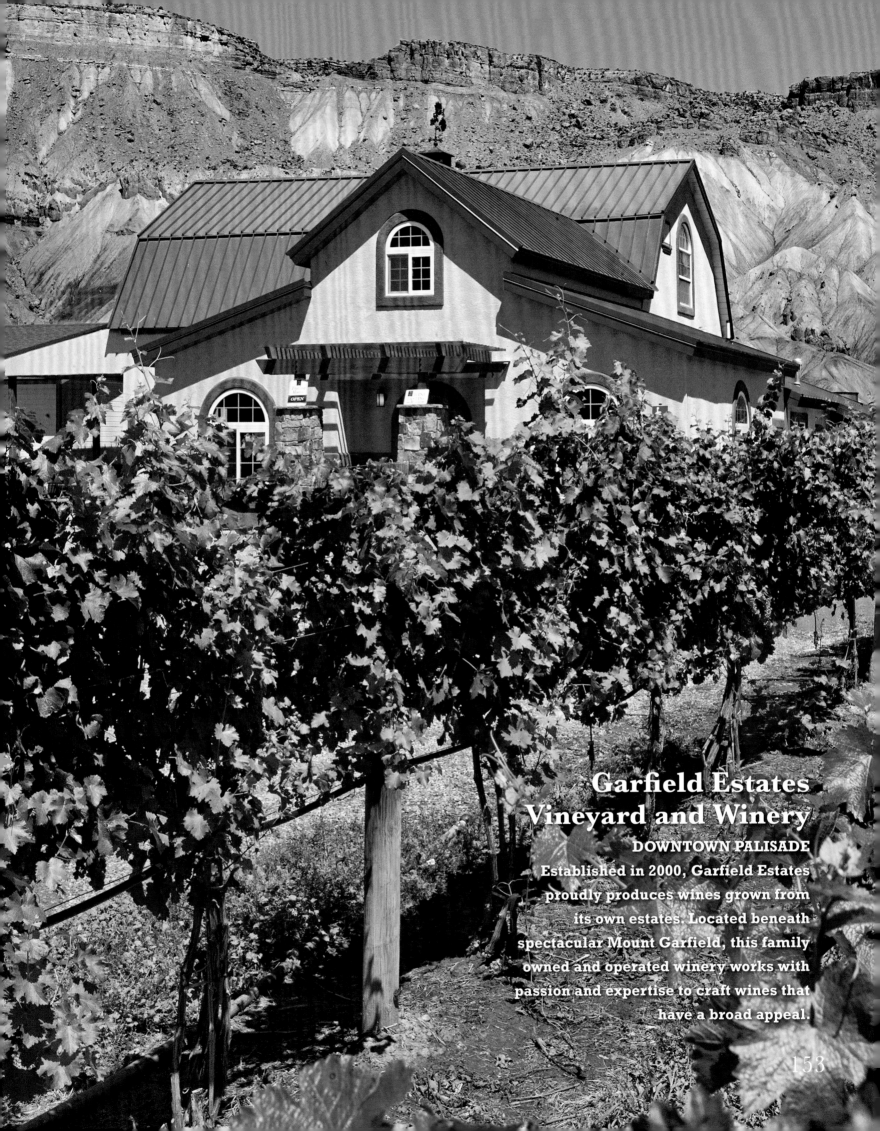

Garfield Estates Vineyard and Winery

DOWNTOWN PALISADE

Established in 2000, Garfield Estates proudly produces wines grown from its own estates. Located beneath spectacular Mount Garfield, this family owned and operated winery works with passion and expertise to craft wines that have a broad appeal.

Tall cottonwood trees line a path along the Colorado River and a quiet pond provides shelter for migratory birds as well as a place for local dogs to cool off with a swim. In the summertime, Palisade residents often head down to Riverbend Park to take a break from the desert heat. The Park features walking trails and a popular 18-hole disc golf course.

Varaison Vineyards

Est. 2004

Molecular gastronomy meets classic wine fermentation at this unconventional winery, where science is used to speed up the aging process and achieve the rich taste experience of Old World wines in a shorter period of time.

A stately Victorian home is the location for this boutique, family-run winery and tasting room. Varaison was founded by Ron and Kristin West, who moved from Denver to the Grand Valley. A chemist by training, Ron is drawn to the Old World style of wine. Today, with the assistance of sons Alex and Andrew, Ron produces classic varietal wines with an emphasis on rich, distinct flavors. The West family prides itself on the unique winetasting experience offered at Varaison.

Owners Ron and Kristin West

Winemakers Ron, Alex and Andrew West

Coordinates 39°6'42.87"N 108°21'21.14"W

Altitude 4,735 ft

Annual Rainfall Liquid precipitation 10.2" (9" rain; 12" snow)

Dominant Soil Type Turley clay loam 2–5% slopes, derived from sandstone and shale

Prominent Wines Bin 3115 Merlot, Crème Brûlée Chardonnay, Nebbiolo, Barbera, Cuvée Blanc Chardonnay, Montagne Doux Viognier, Cuvée Noir Black Muscato Rosé, Crème l'Orange Chardonnay/Orange Muscato Sweet Wine, Forbidden Fruit Hard Ciders

Annual Production 4,000 cases

Wine Tasting Available Daily, 10am to 5pm

Restaurant 13° Brix Cider Bistro

Website www.varaisonvineyards.com

Palisade's main thoroughfare is lined with elegant homes from the Victorian era. And it is here, adjacent to the West family's expansive rose garden, that the Varaison Vineyards tasting room is located. Built in 1904, the home was occupied by a single family from the 1930s until 2004. In 2004, the property was purchased by the Wests, and the home was painstakingly restored to its original condition.

The Wests have carefully preserved many of the documents and artifacts discovered during the home's renovation. Today visitors to the tasting room can experience a journey through the past century in the framed periodicals displayed throughout the tasting room, recording events from the sinking of the *Titanic* to the celebrations at the end of World War II.

Varaison's Victorian tasting room is filled with antiques, polished wood accents, and a private underground dining room and wine cellar. Owner Ron West uses the wine thief to sample a new vintage in the cellar (first spread); *Ron West and son Andrew inspect vines in the family vineyard* (left page). *Kristin West* (above) *at the bar that was custom made for the tasting room. Son Alex* (below) *gives his full attention to the fragrance of a Nebbiolo. States Alex, "The wine experience at Varaison extends beyond the lip of the glass."*

You read about Absolute Prestige Limousine Service on page 91 – the go-to-guys for luxurious wine country tours. However, there are some that yearn for something of the old-fashioned, romantic and carbon-footprint-friendly (and might we say, with a little more horsepower) variety. Absolute Prestige offers horse-drawn carriages, led by majestic teams of black or grey Percherons, or Sorrel Belgians. It's a hit for special occasions, a stately tour of the historic downtown and Colorado River, or simply for a delightful spot of the whimsical. Hint: You can thank your team of horses with a treat of carrot or apple from the local farmers' market.

The Wine Country Inn

777 Grande River Drive, Palisade

An expansive, Victorian-style hotel, beneath the majestic Book Cliffs and surrounded by 21 acres of working vineyards, the Wine Country Inn is the premier location from which to explore the Grand Valley's wine country.

Back in the 1990s, as Palisade's wine production began to pick up speed, Richard and Jean Tally were approached by local winemakers with the idea of creating a lodging choice to serve the growing number of visitors to the area. The Tallys were intrigued, and spent the next several years traveling in Europe and throughout California's wine country, taking notes on which hotels seemed to best serve groups of wine travelers. They would model their Wine Country Inn after those that beautifully blended a respect for the history of the location and the agricultural flavor of the community, with food, wine, and travel.

In 2006, Steve Smith of Grande River Vineyards put a portion of his property up for sale, and the Tallys jumped at the opportunity to acquire this gorgeous vineyard acreage. In 2007, ground was broken for the new Wine Country Inn, which officially opened its doors on August 1st 2008, and since that time, 18 more acres of vineyard have been acquired. Today, The Wine Country Inn and Grande River Vineyards work together cooperatively, with Grande River producing wines from the vineyards now owned by the Tallys, with private labeling wine for The Wine Country Inn.

(Right) *Today Jean and Richard modestly refer to the inn as a "mom and pop" operation. Daughter Anne is Assistant General Manager and is co-owner along with her brother, Greg.*

"Two generations of Tallys have shepherded this project. We are so grateful to have our children helping us."

In Palisade, farm-to-table is a way of life. And in keeping with the agricultural flavor of the community, the Wine Country Inn sources most of its produce from local farms – as well as from its own extensive kitchen garden. Peppers of all varieties, luscious tomatoes, cucumbers, onions and savory herbs are all just a few steps from the kitchen – and the table – thanks to gardener Ebadio Diaz.

General Manager, Ian Kelley (opposite top right) *is the backbone of the operation.*

This lovely 80-room inn has been carefully designed and constructed so that it feels like it belongs in Palisade. Jean Tally refers to the style as "Victorian Farmhouse Vernacular", with wraparound porches, gables, and wood siding.

With its spectacular vineyard setting, the Inn is a favorite venue for special, lifetime events. An open-air pavilion is a gracious space, beneath the towering Book Cliffs, for weddings or other important moments.

The Wine Country Inn is also one of the most sought after dining locations in the Grand Valley. Guests to the Inn will enjoy a complimentary glass of the Inn's private label wine, made from grapes grown in its own vineyards. Dinner choices are crafted from the freshest local ingredients by chef extraordinaire David Kassera. Signature menu items include Caprese salad made with tomatoes from the Inn's own gardens; pan-seared and oven-roasted Colorado lamb chops; and peach bread pudding made with Palisade's favorite fruit.

Colorado National Monument

One of the most magnificent landscapes of the American West is found just outside of Grand Junction, in the Colorado National Monument. Here are geological formations that are estimated to be over 150 million years old: towering stone spires, immense arches, and dizzying expanses of red rock canyon. The 23-mile Rim Rock Drive through the monument climbs 2,000 feet up from the valley and is quite literally breathtaking: you may need to stop and catch your breath as the route twists upward through hairpin turns and tunnels and continues on along the rim of precipitously steep cliffs. The drive reaches its highest point at an elevation of 6,640 feet, overlooking Ute Canyon.

As a National Park, the Colorado National Monument came about because of the dream of one eccentric and determined individual: John Otto. Born in Missouri, Otto first discovered these canyons in 1906, writing: "I came here last year and found these canyons, and they feel like the heart of the world to me. I'm going to stay and build trails and promote this place, because it should be a national park." Otto lived alone in the canyons, using a pickax to carve out trails. Though reclusive, he also took opportunities to publicize the canyons, speaking to reporters, photographers and public officials whenever he could. His enthusiasm caught on and eventually others in the Grand Valley took up his cause, petitioning Washington to preserve the area as a National Park. In May 1911, President Taft signed a proclamation that established the Colorado National Monument.

Creatures leaping, crawling, and flying make the Monument their home: golden eagles and red-tailed hawks soar above the canyons; mule deer and bighorn sheep pick their way nimbly along narrow cliffs. And darting among rocks and boulders are the desert cottontail rabbit and several species of lizard. With patience and luck, the visitor may be rewarded with a glimpse of these elusive desert inhabitants.

COKE OVENS, MONUMENT CANYON
One of the most iconic scenes within the Colorado National Monument is the view of the ancient eroding sandstone monoliths, the Coke Ovens in Monument Canyon (*seen here*). Hiking trails winding through Monument Canyon offer views of the Coke Ovens as well as the Kissing Couple, Praying Hands, and Independence Monument (*previous page*), where each year the American flag is planted on Independence Day by intrepid climbers.

RODEO!

Cowboys and cowgirls busting broncs, riding bulls, wrestling steer, and roping calves. In Colorado, rodeo is a year-round activity in towns big and small throughout the state. The National Western Stock Show and Rodeo is the largest rodeo in Colorado, and takes place in Denver during the month of January. All summer long, weekly rodeos in Mesa County (*shown here*) attract local and national pros to compete at daring feats of riding, roping, and wrestling. There's even a competition for the youngest cowboys and cowgirls in training – mutton busting atop a woolly, rambunctious sheep! While rodeos are a family event, bursting with fun and fanfare, they are also a celebration and homage to Colorado's Wild West heritage and that legendary figure: the Cowboy. Cowboys (and cowgirls) continue to play an important role on ranches and farms throughout the state, and the cowboy culture is very much alive and well in Colorado.

Before the rodeo begins, with its challenges, excitement, and dangers, many a bronc buster will pause to say the Cowboy Prayer:

"Cowboys do not ask for special favors. We do ask Lord, that you will help us live our lives here on earth as Cowboys, in such a manner that when we make that last inevitable ride, to the country up there, where the grass grows lush, green, and stirrup high, and the water runs cool, clear, and deep, that you, as our last Judge, will take us by the hand and say – Welcome to Heaven Cowboy, your entry fees are paid."

— ROCKY MOUNTAINS —

The Rocky Mountains is a massive, 3,000-mile mountain chain extending from Alaska, through Canada, and traversing the western half of the United States into New Mexico. Most of the southern Rocky Mountains fall within the State of Colorado, with Colorado's Mount Elbert being the highest peak in the entire range at 14,440 feet. Colorado's Rocky Mountain wine region stretches from Glenwood Springs to the west, Aspen to the south, Steamboat Springs to the north, and Fraser to the east. It is a region that is famous for its world-class ski resorts, such as Aspen, Vail, Steamboat Springs, Breckenridge, and Winter Park. Singer John Denver may have planted Colorado into our modern, collective consciousness with his song *Rocky Mountain High*. For many, the quintessential Colorado experience is a trip to the Colorado Rockies – to hike the 14,000-foot peaks, ski through knee-high powder amid the vast mountain bowls, explore historic mining towns, or whitewater raft down the Colorado River. Many of the now famous locations in this region – Aspen, Breckenridge, Frisco, Steamboat – began as mining towns in the 19th century and were established through the grit and tenacity of early prospectors who moved west with the dream of making their fortunes in silver and gold. The next wave of hardy risk-takers were those in the 20th century who recognized in the high-peaked terrain the possibility of creating ski resorts to rival those in Europe. A love of adventure, experimentation and reinvention are all qualities that characterize those who are drawn to the Rocky Mountains. There are no vineyards in the Rocky Mountains, where snow can dominate the landscape even into July. Nonetheless, adventurous winemakers are emerging throughout the region, sourcing grapes from Colorado's Grand Valley as well as from California, to be crushed, pressed, and fermented on site. And it is here in the Rocky Mountains where a visitor's first introduction to Colorado wine is often made. After a day on the ski slopes, or shooting the rapids, the curious wine enthusiast may order that first glass of Colorado wine, sparking a desire to learn more about Colorado's wine country.

{
A spirit of adventure defines the Rocky Mountains, and is expressed in world-class skiing, whitewater rafting, and a new culture of innovative winemaking. For many, the high peaks of the Rocky Mountains are the quintessential Colorado experience – and a first introduction to Colorado wines.
}

Outdoor enthusiasts flock to Breckenridge year round for winter and summer activities that go well beyond skiing and snowboarding! Summer in the mountains brings performance series' by two orchestras, as well as multiple outdoor art programs dreamed up by the Breckenridge Creative Arts organization. Breckenridge is home to several breweries, the Breckenridge Distillery (producer of the nationally distributed Breckenridge Bourbon), and a new Colorado winery. Here in "Breck", there are plenty of opportunities to enjoy the high life!

Rocky Mountain High

Wine travelers visiting the Rocky Mountain region will want to explore the mountain resort towns of Vail, in Eagle County, and Breckenridge and Frisco, in nearby Summit County. Founded in 1962 and created in the style of an alpine village, Vail is one of the premier ski resorts in the world and sits at an elevation of 8,022 feet. More recently, Vail and nearby Beaver Creek have increased their offerings of spring and summer activities, now attracting visitors year-round. Vail hosts The Taste of Vail, an annual multiday food and winetasting extravaganza. The Philadelphia Orchestra and New York Philharmonic make Vail their summer home, with concerts given from June through August. Vail is also the location of the busy regional Eagle Vail Airport.

Further east and up at 9,600 feet lies the town of Breckenridge and neighboring Frisco. Both were originally established in the 19th century as mining towns, and today still maintain their classic western ambience. Like its neighbor Vail, Breckenridge is home to world-class skiing at Breckenridge Mountain Resort. And nearby Keystone, Copper Mountain, and Arapahoe Basin offer even more choices to the ski enthusiast. When summer comes to the region, locals and visitors enjoy hiking, mountain biking, and kayaking on Lake Dillon Reservoir, as well as regular music performances and festivals. The fall Breckenridge Wine Classic is another must-stop on the wine traveler's itinerary.

If landing that monster trout is on your bucket list, The Blue River in Summit County is the go-to destination for fly-fishing. The "Blue" fishes well from March through November; book a local guide to lead you to your trouts' favorite hiding spots!

Curious and always on the alert, the lovely mule deer gets its name from its unusually large, mule-like ears. The Rocky Mountain columbine is the state flower of Colorado – admire its beautiful lavender and white blossoms, but leave it unharmed in its natural setting!

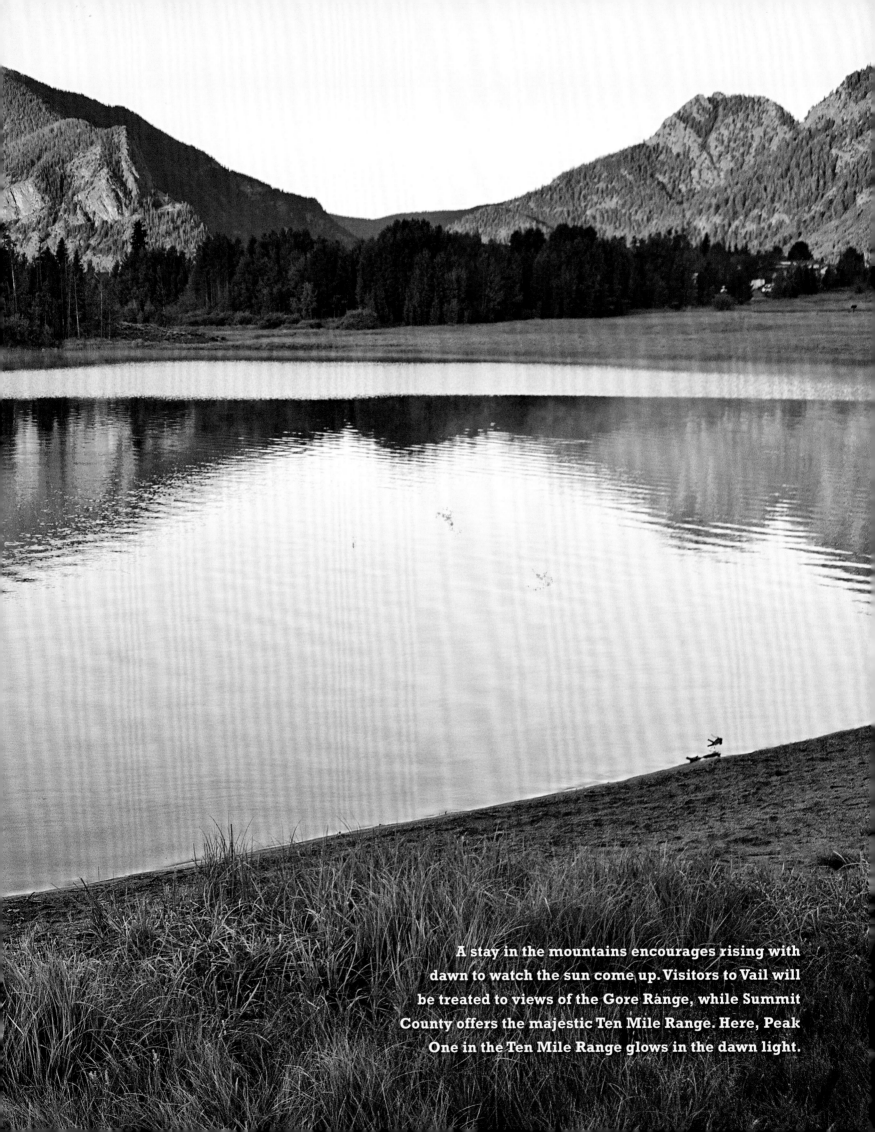

A stay in the mountains encourages rising with dawn to watch the sun come up. Visitors to Vail will be treated to views of the Gore Range, while Summit County offers the majestic Ten Mile Range. Here, Peak One in the Ten Mile Range glows in the dawn light.

Dinners, wine tastings, and other special events are held in the wine cellar and on the outdoor patio at Vines at Vail Winery.

Vines at Vail Winery

WOLCOTT, EAGLE COUNTY

Owner and winemaker Patrick Chirichillo has
a way of welcoming every visitor to Vines at
Vail Winery like a long-lost friend. Raised in an
Italian–American family where he participated
in making the family wine from the age of
nine, Patrick produces his wine from grapes
grown in Northern Central Valley, California.
Prominent varietals include Petite Sirah,
Old Vine Zinfandel, Barbera, and Cabernet
Sauvignon. Tasty blends like Vail Bella and Vail
Ink are also customer favorites.
Vines at Vail Winery, established in 1991, is at
an altitude of 7,200 feet. The winery is located
at 4 Eagle Ranch, a Western-style ranch setting
which features outdoor adventure activities
from horseback riding to ATV tours, zip lining,
jeep tours and glamping – glamorous camping.
Stop by for a glass of wine with Patrick. Cheers!

189

" When David first arrived in Frisco, Main Street was a dirt road. He came to be a ski bum, but fell in love with cooking. "

Food Hedz World Café

842 Summit Boulevard, Frisco

Five-star chef David Welch has earned a loyal following of foodies, thanks to his dedication to sourcing the freshest ingredients from his network of top quality suppliers – from within Colorado and across the globe.

Food Hedz World Café was born out of chef David Welch's desire to *get closer*: to those who are enjoying his food, and to where that food is coming from. Welch arrived in Colorado at the age of 17 with the intention of being a ski bum. He took a job in a local resort restaurant to support himself, and to his surprise fell in love instantly with cooking. Outdoor adventure took a backseat and David worked his way up the ladder, eventually landing the position of Executive Chef at the five star-rated Keystone Ranch in Keystone, Colorado. Today David and his wife, Patti, place a premium on knowing who is producing the ingredients they use, and they source those ingredients directly: an extensive network of local Colorado suppliers work on a regular basis with Food Hedz. When more

exotic ingredients are called for, David picks up the phone and has fish flown in from Hawaii, or a particular batch of salad greens delivered from California. Fresh bread is baked daily and David makes his own soup stocks from scratch. When it comes to wine, the Welches always offer a Colorado selection. In demand throughout the Rocky Mountain towns of Breckenridge and Frisco, Food Hedz World Café operates a busy, full-service catering business. David and his team bring their talents and outstanding menu to events large or small, corporate or private – and will also host dinners and parties in their own French farmhouse-style location in Frisco. David has been voted Chef-of-the-Year by the Colorado Hotel and Lodging Association and has been awarded Zagat's No. 1 rating as chef three years in a row.

Whitewater rafting is high on the list for visitors to Colorado, and the Rocky Mountain region has some of the most challenging and exciting stretches of rapids. The Shoshone Rapids of the Colorado River follow a dramatic course through Glenwood Canyon, and include such highlights as Baptism, Tuttle's Tumble, Tombstone (*shown here*), the Wall, and Maneater.

Wild Women Winery

THE FRONT RANGE

The wine region referred to as the Front Range stretches as far north as Rocky Mountain National Park, east to the plains, and then heads south towards Colorado Springs. At the center of this region is the eclectic, tradition-busting urban wine scene of Denver. The majority of Colorado's wine grapes are produced in the vineyards of Grand Valley; very few winemakers on the Front Range are involved in growing their own grapes. Yet, paradoxically, one might say that Colorado's modern wine industry began in the urban heart of Denver. Prohibition in the 1920s forced early Coloradan winemakers to uproot their vineyards and replace them with other crops. It was not until the 1960s that wine production in Colorado was to get a second chance. Some of the colorful personalities involved in the pioneering efforts to bring grape growing back to Colorado were a Denver dentist and part-time wine enthusiast named Gerald Ivancie, and a young winemaker from California, Warren Winiarski. Ivancie had a successful wine business using grapes shipped to Denver from California, but he wanted to produce grapes closer by, in Colorado. Initiatives launched by Denver-based wine enthusiasts that would have lasting success creating wine with grapes grown in Colorado, and which are still in operation today, include Colorado Mountain Vineyards (which would later evolve into Colorado Cellars), Plum Creek Winery, Grande River Vineyards, and Carlson Vineyards. Today visitors to Colorado's Front Range will find a wide range of wine drinking experiences to explore. Winemakers like Julie Balistreri and Doug Kingman have strong connections to very specific Colorado vineyards and work hand-in-hand with favorite growers. Other wineries source grapes from California and Oregon, as well as from Colorado. Some, like Wild Women Winery (*left*) even offer customers the opportunity to mix their own personal "blends". One of Colorado's most well-known wineries, The Infinite Monkey Theorem, has attracted a growing audience of wine drinkers with what some would call sacrilege – and others, perfect for a Colorado rafting trip – wine in cans.

{ *Anything goes on the Front Range: while some winemakers proudly create wines made from grapes grown only in Colorado, others blend wines from different sources. Ideal for Colorado's outdoor lifestyle, backpack-friendly wine-in-cans is the newest rage.* }

In and around Denver, wine enthusiasts have access to dozens of wineries. Balistreri Vineyards and Doug Kingman Estates are two popular choices for visitors and locals; The Infinite Monkey Theorem has gained notoriety for its packaging of wine in cans. Creekside Cellars, in the suburb of Evergreen, serves award-winning wines made by winemaker Michelle Cleveland in a shady setting overlooking Bear Creek.

The Colorado Wine Governor's Cup Competition
Each summer an esteemed panel of judges gathers to taste submissions from some of Colorado's more than 140 different producers of wines, ciders, meads, and fruit wines. *Facing page, from left to right*, Colorado Governor John Hickenlooper presents the 2016 Governor's Cup Award to Glenn Foster of Meadery of the Rockies for Best-in-Show Honey Wine and John Garlich of Bookcliff Vineyards for Best-in-Show Grape Wine. Doug Caskey of the Colorado Wine Industry Development Board congratulates the winners.

Balistreri Vineyards

Est. 1998

The Balistreri family makes a point of encouraging guests to feel right at home at this stylish urban winery, where over 20 wine selections can be enjoyed at the expansive bar, or paired with seasonally inspired appetizers or lunch.

Guests visiting the tasting room are likely to be served by founder John Balistreri, and led through a tasting of some of his favorite varietals. Balistreri is clearly proud of his wine, and equally proud of the family that surrounds him and has been instrumental in creating Balistreri Vineyard's success – from daughter Julie who runs the day-to-day operations and joins her father in winemaking, to John's wife Birdie; altogether three generations of Balistreri family create this uniquely welcoming winetasting experience.

Owners John, Birdie and Julie Balistreri

Winemaker John Balistreri

Viticulturists John and Julie Balistreri

Coordinates 39°48'57.1"N 104°57'52.4"W

Altitude 4,728 ft

Annual Rainfall Liquid precipitation 11.2" (10" rain; 12" snow)

Dominant Soil Type Clay loam

Annual Production 7,000 to 8,000 cases

Wine Tasting Available Year-round, except for Thanksgiving, Christmas, New Year's Day, and Easter

Notable Awards At the Denver International Wine Festival, Gold medals for the 2015 Sangiovese and 2013 Colorado Syrah from Horse Mountain Vineyard

Restaurant Same as tasting room 11-5

Website www.balistrerivineyards.com

199

Like many Italian families, every generation of Balistreri has produced wine for the consumption of family and friends. In 1998, at the urging of his wife Birdie and daughter Julie, John Balistreri (left, seated at the bar) built a modest tasting room on their Denver farm property to showcase the family wine and offer it to the public.

Demand for Balistreri wine grew to the point where the family made the decision to build a spacious tasting room, restaurant and event space.

Today Balistreri produces nearly 8,000 cases of wine a year and welcomes visitors from across the country. The on-site gourmet kitchen, excellent restaurant, and large event space makes Balistreri a popular choice for important business and family occasions.

Creativity expresses itself in many forms at Balistreri; son John and grandson John Domenico are both sculptors, with works on display inside the tasting room and out in the garden. The sculpture shown at left is the work of Julie's son, John Domenico.

Who goes there? In the high country of Colorado, the watchful marmot calls out the alarm with a high-pitched whistle. The sturdy and sociable marmot (seen here at 14,130 feet on the Front Range's Mount Evans Scenic Byway) also goes by the less dignified name of "whistlepig". Related to the marmot is Colorado's golden-mantled ground squirrel. Campers or hikers should not be surprised by the appearance of this inquisitive, chipmunk-like rodent who often shows up as soon as the picnic is laid out.

Kingman Estates Winery

Est. 2011

"It's Wine O'Clock!" owner and winemaker Doug Kingman likes to say, encouraging wine connoisseurs and curious newcomers to join him for a glass at Kingman Estates' hip tasting room in downtown Denver.

K ingman Estates has been quickly accumulating awards for its pleasingly structured Cabernet Sauvignons and Cabernet Francs. All grapes are grown in Colorado's Grand Valley, and de-stemmed, crushed and bottled at Kingman's Denver location with the help of an enthusiastic band of volunteers. Visitors to the winery sit among barrels of red wine that line the tasting room. Sixteen varietals are offered, and light fare is also available. Currently producing 3,500 cases of wine a year, Kingman has aggressive plans to grow that output to 10,000 cases per year.

Owners Doug and Karen Kingman

Winemaker Doug Kingman

Viticulturist Varies by vineyard; all grapes are purchased from independent Colorado growers

Coordinates 39°48'44.5"N 104°58'33.1"W

Altitude 4,790 ft

Annual Rainfall Liquid precipitation 11.2" (10" rain; 12" snow)

Dominant Soil Type Varies by vineyard

Prominent Wines Cabernet Sauvignon, Cabernet Franc, Merlot, Tempranillo, Marquette, Riesling, Viognier, Chardonnay, and La Crescent

Annual Production 3,500 cases

Wine Tasting Available Saturday and Sunday from 12pm to 5pm

Restaurant Light fare available

Notable Awards Gold medals in 2016 for 2013 Cabernet Sauvignon and Cabernet Franc; 87 Points in 2015 from *Wine Spectator* for 2012 Cabernet Sauvignon; Best of Colorado Mountain Festival award for 2010 Cabernet Sauvignon in 2012

Website www.kingmanwine.com

WHERE THE BUFFALO STILL ROAM

Direct descendants of the last wild herd of bison in America, Denver's herd of two dozen buffalo roams freely in a large natural preserve west of the city. The herd has grown and flourished in their urban pastureland of grass and pine trees. Watching over the herd, perhaps, is the spirit of Buffalo Bill Cody, whose final resting place is just up the road, on Lookout Mountain.

208

Winery Listing

THE FOUR CORNERS

FOUR LEAVES WINERY
528 Main Avenue, Durango, CO 81301
Tel: 970-403-8182
Email: dean@winerymsprings.com
www.fourleaveswinery.com

FOX FIRE FARMS
5513 CO Road 321, Ignacio, CO 81137
Tel: 970-563-4675
Email: richard@foxfirefarms.com
www.foxfirefarms.com

GUY DREW VINEYARDS
19891 County Road G, Cortez, CO 81321
Tel: 970-403-8182
Email: guydrew@q.com
www.guydrewvineyards.com

GUY DREW TASTING ROOM
Ute Mountain Indian Trading Co.,
27601 US 160, Cortez, CO 81321
Email: guydrew@q.com
www.guydrewvineyards.com

SUTCLIFFE VINEYARDS ★
12174 County Road G, Cortez, CO 81321
Tel: 970-565-0825
Email: info@sutcliffewines.com
www.sutcliffewines.com

WEST ELKS

ALFRED EAMES CELLARS ★
11931 4050 Road, Paonia, CO 81428
Tel: 970-527-3269
Email: alfredeamescellars@gmail.com
www.alfredeamescellars.com

AZURA
16764 Farmers Mine Road, Paonia,
CO 81428
Tel: 970-390-4251
Email: azurapaonia@aol.com
www.azuracellars.com

BIG B'S HARD CIDER ★
39126 Highway 133, Hotchkiss, CO 81419
Tel: 970-527-1110
Email: info@bigbs.com
www.bigbs.com

BLACK BRIDGE
15836 Black Bridge Road, Paonia,
CO 81428
Tel: 970-527-6838
Email: leeb@orchardvalleyfarms.com
www.orchardvalleyfarms.com

FIRE MOUNTAIN VINEYARD
38594 Stucker Mesa Road, Hotchkiss,
CO 81419
Tel: 970-433-5323
Email: firemountainvineyard@skybeam.
com

JACK RABBIT HILL
26567 North Road, Hotchkiss, CO 81419
Tel: 970-835-3677
Email: lance@jackrabbithill.com
www.jackrabbithill.com

LEROUX CREEK VINEYARDS ★
12388 3100 Road, Hotchkiss, CO 81419
Tel: 970-872-4746
Email: lerouxcreekinn@msn.com
www.lerouxcreekinn.com

MESA WINDS FARM AND WINERY
31262 L Road, Hotchkiss, CO 81419
Tel: 970-250-4788
Email: mail@mesawindsfarm.com
www.mesawindsfarm.com

STONE COTTAGE CELLARS
41716 Reds Road, Paonia, CO 81428
Tel: 970-527-3444
Email: info@stonecottagecellars.com
www.stonecottagecellars.com

TERROR CREEK WINERY ★
17445 Garvin Mesa Road, Paonia,
CO 81428
Tel: 970-527-3484
Email: jmath@paonia.com
www.terrorcreekwinery.com

DELTA & MONTROSE

COTTONWOOD CELLARS
5482 Hwy 348, Olathe, CO 81425
Tel: 970-323-6224
Email: cowinelady@cs.com
www.cottonwoodcellars.com

CRAG CREST CELLARS ★
24621 Tannin Road, Cedaredge,
CO 81413
Tel: 303-518-0581
Email: davesorchard@gmail.com
www.cragcrestcellars.com

EDGE OF CEDARS FARM & WINERY
250 SW 7th Street, Cedaredge, CO 81413
Tel: 970-623-9189
Email: edgeofcedarsfarm@gmail.com
www.thewineryatcedarsfarm.com

GARRETT ESTATES CELLARS
53582 Falcon Road, Olathe, CO 81425
Tel: 970-901-5919
Email: mitch@garrettestatecellars.com
www.garrettestatecellars.com

MOUNTAIN VIEW WINERY
5859 5825 Road, Olathe, CO 81425
Tel: 970-323-6816
Email: mountainviewwinery@gmail.com
www.mountainviewwinery.com

STONEY MESA WINERY
16199 Happy Hollow Road, Cedaredge,
CO 81413
Tel: 970-856-9463
Email: wine@stoneymesa.com
www.stoneymesa.com

WOODY CREEK CELLARS
150 SW 5th Street, Cedaredge, CO 81413
Tel: 970-901-7575
Email: dtourney@tds.net
www.woodycreekcellars.com

GRAND VALLEY

AVANT VINEYARDS
3480 E Road, Palisade, CO 81526
Tel: 970-216-9908
Email: avantvineyards@aol.com

CARLSON VINEYARDS ★
461 35 Road, Palisade, CO 81526
Tel: 888-464-5444
Email: info@carlsonvineyards.com
www.carlsonvineyards.com

COLORADO CELLARS WINERY ★
3553 E Road, Palisade, CO 81526
Tel: 800-848-2812
Email: info@coloradocellars.com
www.coloradocellars.com

COLTERRIS WINERY ON NORTH RIVER ROAD ★
3907 N River Rd, Palisade, CO 81526
Tel: 970-464-1150
Email: theresa@colterris.com
www.colterris.com

COLTERRIS AT THE OVERLOOK ★
3548 E 1/2 Road, Palisade, CO 81526
Tel: 970-464-1150
Email: theresa@colterris.com
www.colterris.com

DEBEQUE CANYON WINERY ★
351 West 8th Street, Palisade, CO 81526
Tel: 970-464-0550
Email: debequecanyonwines@bresnan.net
www.debequecanyonwinery.com

DESERT SUN VINEYARDS
3230 B 1/2 Road, Grand Junction, CO 81503
Tel: 970-434-9851
Email: desertsunvineyards@bresnan.net
www.desertsunvineyards.com

GARFIELD ESTATES VINEYARD AND WINERY ★
3572 G Road, Palisade, CO 81526
Tel: 970-464-0941
Email: info@garfieldestates.com
www.garfieldestates.com

GRANDE RIVER VINEYARDS ★
787 N. Elberta Avenue, Palisade, CO 81526
Tel: 1-800-CO-GROWN
Email: info@granderiverwines.com
www.granderivervineyards.com

GRAYSTONE WINERY ★
3352 F Road, Clifton, CO 81520
Tel: 970-434-8610
Email: sales@graystonewines.com
www.graystonewines.com

GUBBINI WINERY
3697 F Road, Palisade, CO 81526
Tel: 970-270-7185
Email: gubbiniwinery@aol.com

HERMOSA VINEYARDS
3269 3/4 C Road, Palisade, CO 81526
Tel: 970-640-0940
Email: hermosavineyards@aol.com
www.hermosavineyards.com

KAHIL WINERY
Grand Junction, CO 81503
Tel: 970-640-3541
Email: kahilwinery@hotmail.com

MAISON LA BELLE VIE
3575 G Road, Palisade, CO 81526
Tel: 970-464-4959
Email: frenchybar@aol.com
www.maisonlabellevie.com

MEADERY OF THE ROCKIES
3701 G Road, Palisade, CO 81526
Tel: 970-464-7899
www.talonwinebrands.com

MESA PARK VINEYARDS
3321 C Road, Palisade, CO 81526
Tel: 970-434-4191
Email: brookerwebb@gmail.com
www.mesaparkvineyards.com

PLUM CREEK CELLARS ★
3708 G Road, Palisade, CO 81526
Tel: 970-464-7586
Email: plumcreekwinery@att.net
www.plumcreekwinery.com

PTARMIGAN VINEYARDS
221 31 3/10 Road, Grand Junction, CO 81503
Tel: 970-434-2015
Email: wine@ptarmiganvineyards.com
www.ptarmiganvineyards.com

RED FOX CELLARS ★
695 36 Road, Unit C, Palisade, CO 81526
Tel: 970-464-1099
Email: info@redfoxcellars.com
www.redfoxcellars.com

REEDER MESA
7799 Reeder Mesa Road, Whitewater, CO 81527
Tel: 970-242-7468
Email: info@reedermesawines.com
www.reedermesawines.com

SUMMIT CELLARS
595 36th Road, Palisade, CO 81526
Tel: 970-361-4980
www.summitcellars@msn.com

TALBOTT'S CIDER COMPANY ★
3801 F 1/4 Road, Palisade, CO 81526
Tel: 970-464-5656
Email: talbottsciderco@gmail.com
www.talbottsciderco.com

TALON WINERY AND ST. KATHERYN'S CELLAR
785 Elberta Avenue, Palisade, CO 81526
Tel: 970-464-1300
www.talonwinebrands.com

TWO RIVERS WINERY ★
2087 Broadway, Grand Junction, CO 81507
Tel: 970-255-1471
Email: info@tworiverswinery.com
www.tworiverswinery.com

VARAISON VINEYARDS AND WINERY ★
405 West First Street, Palisade, CO 81526
Tel: 970-464-4928
Email: info@varaisonvineyards.com
www.varaisonvineyards.com

WHITEWATER HILL VINEYARDS
220 32 Road, Grand Junction, CO 81503
Tel: 970-434-6868
Email: info@whitewaterhill.com
www.whitewaterhill.com

ROCKY MOUNTAINS

CONTINENTAL DIVIDE WINERY
505 South Main Street, Breckenridge, CO 80424
Tel: 970-771-3443
Email: jeffrey@breckwinery.com
www.breckwinery.com

MINTURN CELLARS
107 Williams Street, Minturn, CO 81645
Tel: 970-827-4065

VINES AT VAIL VALLEY ★
4 Eagle Ranch, 4098 Highway 131, Wolcott, CO 81655
Tel: 970-949-9463
Email: patrick@vinesatvailwinery.com
www.vinesatvailwinery.com

WINTER PARK WINERY
395 Zerex Street, Fraser, CO 80442
Tel: 970-726-4514
Email: jon@winterparkwinery.com
www.winterparkwinery.com

THE FRONT RANGE

ALLIS RANCH WINERY
901 Allis Ranch Road, Sedalia, CO 80135
Tel: 303-881-1294
Email: allisranchwine@gmail.com
www.allisranchwine.com

ASPEN PEAK CELLARS
60750 US Hwy 285, Baily, CO 80421
Tel: 303-816-5504
Email: info@aspenpeakcellars.com
www.aspenpeakcellars.com

AUGUSTINA'S WINERY
20 East Lakeview Drive, Nederland,
CO 80466
Tel: 303-520-4871
Email: augustinaswinery@gmail.com
www.augustinaswinery.com

BAD BITCH CELLARS
15090 Lansing Street, Brighton,
CO 80602
Tel: 303-807-3906
Email: tkkernan@comcast.net
www.badbitchcellars.com

BALISTRERI VINEYARDS ★
1946 E. 66th Avenue, Denver, CO 80229
Tel: 303-287-5156
Email: info@balistreriwine.com
www.balistrerivineyards.com

BLACK ARTS CELLARS
11616 Shaffer Place, Littleton, CO 80127
Tel: 303-722-0669
Email: info@bacellars.com
www.bacellars.com

BLUE MOUNTAIN VINEYARDS
4480 Hoot Owl Drive, Berthoud,
CO 80513
Tel: 970-480-7778
Email: bill@coloradobluemountain.com
www.coloradobluemountain.com

BOOKCLIFF VINEYARDS
1501 Lee Hill Drive, Boulder, CO 80304
Tel: 303-449-9463
Email: winery@bookcliffvineyards.com
www.bookcliffvineyards.com

CLAREMONT INN AND WINERY
800 Claremont Drive, Stratton, CO 80836
Tel: 888-291-8910
Email: claremontinnco@aol.com
www.claremontinn.com

CREEKSIDE CELLARS
28036 Hwy 74, Evergreen, CO 80439
Tel: 303-674-5460
Email: info@creeksidecellars.net
www.creeksidecellars.net

FORGOTTEN ROOTS
624 Main Street, Windsor, CO
Tel: 970-686-5301
Email: info@forgottenrootswinery.com
www.forgottenrootswinery.com

INVINTIONS
9608 East Arapahoe Road, Greenwood
Village, CO 80112
Tel: 303-799-9463
Email: info@invintionswinery.com
www.invintionswinery.com

KINGMAN ESTATES WINERY ★
800 East 64th Avenue, Denver, CO 80229
Tel: 720-560-7270
Email: doug.kingman@kingmanwine.
com
www.kingmanwine.com

LEAP OF FAITH WINERY
11467 West I-70 Frontage Road North,
Wheat Ridge, CO 80033
Tel: 720-484-6685
Email: sky@rmbc.us
www.leapoffaithwinery.com

LEGACY WINERY AND VINEYARDS
5728 S. Rapp Street, Littleton, CO 80120
Tel: 303-798-0196
Email: info@legacywineryandvineyard.
com
www.legacywineryandvineyard.com

LOST PRAIRIE WINERY
251 Jefferson Street, Fort Collins,
CO 80524
Tel: 970-407-9463
Email: lostprairiewinery@gmail.com
www.lostprairiewinery.com

MUMMY HILL WINERY
51368 Hwy 385, Holyoke, CO 80734
Tel: 970-630-1457
Email: dee.blecha@gmail.com
www.mummyhillwinery.com

POINT BLANK WINERY
6547 South Racine Circle, Centennial,
CO 80111
Tel: 720-328-2513
Email: drinkwhatyoulike@
pointblankwinery.com
www. pointblankwinery.com

PURGATORY CELLARS WINERY
18921 Plaza Drive, Parker, CO 80134
Tel: 303-600-8209
Email: info@purgatorycellars.net
www.purgatorycellarscolorado.com

RIVER GARDEN WINERY
9490 County Road 25, Fort Lupton,
CO 80621
Tel: 303-304-4064
Email: rgwinery@gmail.com
www.rivergardenwinery.com

RUBY TRUST CELLARS
864 West Happy Canyon Road, Castle
Rock, CO 80108
Tel: 720-202-2041
Email: info@rubytrustcellars.com
www.rubytrustcellars.com

RYKER'S CELLARS
4640 Pecos Street, Denver, CO 80211
Tel: 720-437-9537
Email: rykerscellars@gmail.com
www.rykerscellars.com

SETTEMBRE CELLARS
1501 Lee Hill Drive, Boulder, CO 80304
Tel: 303-532-1892
Email: contact@settembrecellars.com
www.settembrecellars.com

SILVER VINES WINERY
7509 Grandview Avenue, Arvada,
CO 80002
Tel: 303-456-5212
Email: winery@silvervineswinery.com
www.silvervineswinery.com

SNOWY PEAKS WINERY
292 Moraine Avenue, Estes Park,
CO 80517
Tel: 970-586-2099
Email: info@snowypeakswinery.com
www.snowypeakswinery.com

SPERO WINERY
3316 West 64th Avenue, Denver,
CO 80221
Tel: 720-519-1506
Email: sperowinery@aol.com
www.sperowinery.biz

STONEBRIDGE FARM WINERY
5169 Ute Highway, Longmont, CO 80503
Tel: 303-823-0975
Email: jmartin@greenspeedisp.net
www.frontrangebackyardviticulture.com

TEN BEARS WINERY
5114 County Road 23E, LaPorte,
CO 80535
Tel: 970-566-4043
Email: tenbearswinery@hotmail.com
www.tenbearswinery.com

THE INFINITE MONKEY THEOREM
3200 Larimer Street, Denver, CO 80205
Tel: 303-736-8376
Email: drink@
theinfinitemonkeytheorem.com
www.theinfinitemonkeytheorem.com

TURQUOISE MESA WINERY
11705 Teller Street, Broomfield,
CO 80020
Tel: 303-653-3822
Email: turquoisemesawinery@gmail.
com
www.turquoisemesawinery.com

VIEWPOINT WINES
3075 Fourmile Canyon Drive, Boulder,
CO 80302
Tel: 303-444-9463
Email: molly@viewpointwines.com
www.viewpointwines.com

VINO PASSARELLI
180 Allison, Lakewood, CO
Tel: 303-483-5279
Email: vinopassarelli@gmail.com
www.vinopassarelli.com

VINTAGES HANDCRAFTED WINES
120 West Olive Street, Fort Collins,
CO 80524
970-535-2426
Email: info@vintageswine.com
www.vintageswine.com

WATER 2 WINE
8130 South University, Centennial, CO
80122
Tel: 720-489-9463
Email: derek@water2wine.us
www.water2wine.com

WATERS EDGE WINERY
2101 East Arapahoe Road, Centennial,
CO 80122
Tel: 720-839-5053
Email: info@wewdenver.com
www.wewdenver.com

WHAT WE LOVE, THE WINERY
1501 Lee Hill Drive, Boulder, CO 80304
Tel: 303-963-6342
Email: info@whatwelove.com
www.whatwelove.com

WILD WOMEN WINERY
1660 Champa, Denver, CO 80202
Tel: 303-534-0788
Email: winery@winerydenver.com
www.winerycolorado.com

PIKES PEAK

BLACK FOREST MEADERY
AND WINERY
6420 Burrows Road, Colorado Springs,
CO 80908
Tel: 719-495-7340
Email: mail@blackforestmeadery.com
www.blackforestmeadery.com

BYERS CELLARS
109 W Galena Avenue, Cripple Creek,
CO 80813
Tel: 303-570-5536
Email: byerscellars@aol.com
www.byerscellars.com

CATRONIA CELLARS
243 North Washington Street,
Monument, CO 80132
Tel: 719-481-3477
Email: woody@catrionacellars.com
www.catrionacellars.com

D'VINE WINE
934 Manitou Avenue, Manitou Springs,
CO 80829
Tel: 719-685-1030
Email: winery@winerymsprings.com
www.winerymsprings.com

LE FUSELIER WINERY
1702 Willow Street, Canon City,
CO 81212
Tel: 719-315-2075
Email: david@coloradograpes.com
www.coloradograpes.com

MOUNTAIN SPIRIT WINERY
15750 County Road 220, Salida,
CO 81201
Tel: 719-539-1175
Email: barkett@mountainspiritwinery.
com
www.mountainspiritwinery.com

SETTE DOLORI
9750 Millard Way, Colorado Springs,
CO 80908
Tel: 719-282-1193
Email: tbiolchini@settedolori.com
www.settedolori.com

SONGBIRD CELLARS
881 Grand Avenue, Beulah, CO 81023
Tel: 719-485-7664
Email: songbirdcellars@yahoo.com
www.songbirdcellars.com

THE WINERY AT PIKES PEAK
4455 Fountain Avenue, Cascade,
CO 80809
Tel: 719-684-8000
Email: thewineryatpikespeak@live.com

TWO BROTHERS VINEYARDS
6755 Shoup Road, Black Forest,
CO 80908
Tel: 719-495-7340
Email: mail@blackforestmeadery.com
www.blackforestmeadery.com

WINERY AT HOLY CROSS ABBEY
3011 East US Hwy 50, Canon City,
CO 81212
Tel: 877-HCA-WINE
Email: info@abbeywinery.com
www.abbeywinery.com

VINO SALIDA WINE CELLARS
10495 CR 120, Poncha Springs,
CO 81242
Tel: 719-539-6299
Email: info@vinosalida.com
www.vinosalida.com

Index

Page numbers in **bold** type indicate photographs.

216